P9-AGU-209
02209930

PSYCHOLOGY AS RELIGION

Psychology as Religion

The Cult of Self-Worship

Paul C. Vitz

SECOND EDITION

WILLIAM B. EERDMANS PUBLISHING COMPANY
GRAND RAPIDS, MICHIGAN

THE PATERNOSTER PRESS
CARLISLE, UK

Copyright © 1977 by Wm. B. Eerdmans Publishing Co.
255 Jefferson Ave. S.E., Grand Rapids, Michigan 49503
Second edition copyright © 1994 by Wm. B. Eerdmans Publishing Co.
All rights reserved

Published jointly 1994 by Wm. B. Eerdmans Publising Co. and
The Paternoster Press
P.O. Box 300, Carlisle, Cumbria CA3 0QS, UK

Printed in the United States of America

Reprinted 1994

Library of Congress Cataloging-in-Publication Data

Vitz, Paul C., 1935
    Psychology as religion: the cult of self-worship / Paul C. Vitz. — 2nd ed.
      p.   cm.
    Includes bibliographical references.
    ISBN 0-8028-0725-9 (pbk.)
      1. Psychology and religion. 2. Psychology — Philosophy. 3. Christianity —
Psychology. 4. Self-worship — Controversial literature.   I. Title.
    BF51.V58   1994
    150'.1 — dc20   94-1721
                                             CIP

British Library Cataloguing in Publication Data

Vitz, Paul C.
    Psychology as Religion: Cult of Self-worship. — 2Rev.ed
    I. Title
    200.19

    ISBN 0-85364-619-8

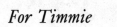

For Timmie

Contents

About This Book

This book is for the reader interested in a critique of contemporary psychology — the reader who knows, perhaps only intuitively, that psychology has become more a sentiment than a science and is now part of the problem of modern life rather than part of its resolution. The varied criticisms offered here are scientific, philosophical, ethical, economic, social, and, finally, religious; their purpose is to provide arguments and concepts that allow the reader to begin the process of placing today's psychology in a much smaller, less corrosive, but ultimately more accurate and more helpful perspective than that which presently prevails.

The first edition of this work — *Psychology as Religion: The Cult of Self-Worship* — came out in 1977 and seems to have been the first book-length critique of the self-worshiping and narcissistic character of so much modern psychology. While it was in press, Tom Wolfe's famous "Me Decade" article appeared.[1] In 1978 Christopher Lasch's best-selling book *The Culture of Narcissism* was published. Lasch brilliantly documented the pervasive egoism and narcissism in modern American society, much of it derived from psychology and other "helping professions." A little later, David G. Myers published his book *The Inflated Self* (1981), which discussed the widespread human tendency — and illusion — to see things as reliably favorable to the self. Success is our achievement; failure is the fault of someone else, or the environment, or bad luck, etc. In 1983, two psychologists, Michael and Lise Wallach, published a systematic critique of all the major theories of psychology since Freud. Their book, *Psychology's Sanction for Selfishness: The Error of Egoism*

---

1. Tom Wolfe, "The 'Me' Decade and the Third Great Awakening," *New York,* 23 Aug. 1976, pp. 26-40.

in Theory and Therapy, showed that all modern psychological theories of human motivation and personality assume that reward for the self (i.e., egoism) is the *only* functional ethical principle. In short, psychology's deep commitment to narcissism, egoism, self-worship, the individual, isolated self—or, as I call it, "selfism"—has been thoroughly demonstrated.[2]

Along with these books came a raft of more general criticisms of psychology, especially psychotherapy. These critiques often ignored the problems of the self to focus on many other weaknesses of psychology. Strong secular criticisms came from Thomas Szasz, *The Myth of Psychotherapy* (1978), Martin L. Gross, *The Psychological Society* (1978), and Bernie Zilbergeld's *The Shrinking of America* (1983). The secular attack on psychology in general has continued unabated through *Psychobabble* (1979) to *Freudian Fraud* (1991). This now powerful critical tradition was begun by Philip Rieff's still well-known *The Triumph of the Therapeutic* (1966).[3]

Meanwhile, Christian critics of psychology also went into high gear. Martin and Deidre Bobgan's *The Psychological Way/The Spiritual Way* (1978) represented an all-out rejection of psychology for Christians. A more scholarly but still very effective critique came from Mary Stewart Van Leeuwen in *The Sorcerer's Apprentice* (1982). W. Kirk Kilpatrick waded in with two popular and insightful critical treatments: *Psychological Seduction* (1982) and *The Emperor's New Clothes* (1985). Sometimes too extreme but usually cogent was Dave Hunt's and T. A. McMahon's best-selling *The Seduction of Christianity* (1985). Don S. Browning came out with *Religious Thought and the Modern Psychologies* (1987), an outstanding and scholarly critical analysis of the ethical and philosophical assumptions made by the major modern psychologies. And religious critiques of psychology are still coming out—for example, Os Guinness

---

2. Christopher Lasch, *The Culture of Narcissism: American Life in an Age of Diminishing Expectations* (New York: Norton, 1978); David G. Myers, *The Inflated Self* (New York: Seabury, 1981); Michael Wallach and Lise Wallach, *Psychology's Sanction for Selfishness: The Error of Egoism in Theory and Therapy* (San Francisco: Freeman, 1983).

3. Thomas Szasz, *The Myth of Psychotherapy: Mental Healing as Religion, Rhetoric, and Repression* (Garden City, NY: Anchor Press/Doubleday, 1978); Martin L. Gross, *The Psychological Society* (New York: Random House, 1978); Bernie Zilbergeld, *The Shrinking of America* (Boston: Little Brown, 1983); Richard D. Rosen, *Psychobabble* (New York: Avon, 1979); Philip Rieff, *The Triumph of the Therapeutic* (New York: Harper & Row, 1966); E. Fuller Torrey, *Freudian Fraud* (New York: Harper Collins, 1992).

and John Seel, *No God but God* (1992). The granddaddy of these Christian critiques is probably Jay Adams's *Competent to Counsel* (1972).[4]

In many ways, then, much has happened to our understanding of psychology since 1977. And yet little has actually changed in how psychology functions in our society, or how it is taught in our colleges and universities. Psychology is probably less talked about in the popular media and somewhat less popular than in the mid-1970s. But we are still very much what Rieff called a "therapeutic society." Self-actualization, self-fulfillment, etc., are standard explanations for the purpose of everything from college education to life itself. Countless Christians worry more about losing their self-esteem than about losing their souls.

In university psychology departments, hundreds of thousands of students every year still take courses in which the books and critical analyses cited above are almost never, if ever, mentioned. Far from being concerned with scholarly and intellectual debate, our psychology departments and their courses focus on supporting the profession, keeping student enrollment up and faculty morale high. Hence there is a need for a new and revised edition of *Psychology as Religion* to make many of the same points as the first edition, but taking into consideration work that has appeared since the book first appeared.

As the title suggests, it will be argued that psychology has become a religion: a secular cult of the self. By this I mean an intensely held worldview, a philosophy of life or ideology. More specifically, contemporary psychology is a form of secular humanism based on the rejection of God and the worship of the self. A good deal of what follows by way of criticism, however, does not presuppose a religious orientation, and devotees of humanistic psychology (e.g., of such concepts as self-actual-

---

4. Martin Bobgan and Deidre Bobgan, *The Psychological Way/The Spiritual Way: Are Christianity and Psychotherapy Compatible?* (Minneapolis: Bethany Fellowship, 1978); Mary Stewart Van Leeuwen, *The Sorcerer's Apprentice: A Christian Looks at the Changing Face of Psychology* (Downers Grove, IL: InterVarsity, 1982); William Kirk Kilpatrick, *Psychological Seduction: The Failure of Modern Psychology* (Nashville: Thomas Nelson, 1982); William Kirk Kilpatrick, *The Emperor's New Clothes* (Westchester, IL: Crossway Books, 1985); D. Hunt and T. A. McMahon, *The Seduction of Christianity: Spiritual Discernment in the Last Days* (Eugene, OR: Harvest House, 1985); Don Browning, *Religious Thought and the Modern Psychologies* (Philadelphia: Fortress, 1987); Os Guinness and John Seel, *No God But God: Breaking with the Idols of Our Age* (Chicago: Moody, 1992); Jay E. Adams, *Competent to Counsel* (Nutley, NJ: Presbyterian and Reformed Publishing Company, 1972).

ization) are challenged to confront a psychologist's criticism of their widely accepted wisdom.

The major critical orientation of this book is Christian. This will be made most explicit in the later chapters. Christianity, like all traditional religions, has a great deal at stake in this discussion. It may be noted that in those cases in which critical arguments are based on Christian theology, my conclusion is usually identical with or close to that which could be made by other theistic religions. The present work is offered in a spirit of cooperation with other faiths, particularly Judaism, in the common struggle against the influence of today's psychology.

Specifically, I shall argue for five theses:

1. Psychology as religion exists, and it exists in strength throughout the United States.
2. Psychology as religion can be criticized on many grounds quite independent of religion.
3. Psychology as religion is deeply anti-Christian.
4. Psychology as religion is extensively supported by schools, universities, and social programs that are financed by taxes collected from millions of Christians. This use of tax money to support what has become a secular ideology raises grave political and legal issues.
5. Psychology as religion has for years been destroying individuals, families, and communities. But in recent years the destructive logic of this secular system is beginning to be understood, and as more and more people discover the emptiness of self-worship Christianity is presented with a major historical opportunity to provide meaning and life.

I make no apology for the intensity of some of my criticism. The issues involved are still only beginning to be acknowledged, and in any case they are very serious. The time has more than come for Christian academics and intellectuals to speak out publicly in defense of the faith, regardless of the professional risk and isolation this may entail. Many of us are in strategic positions to observe and analyze anti-Christian trends in society that escape the theologians, who are often so secularized in today's seminaries that they would be the last to notice.

*　　*　　*

Here a few autobiographical words are in order.[5] Much of the subsequent analysis comes directly out of my personal experience as a student and as an academic psychologist during the last thirty-five years. I was an undergraduate at the University of Michigan from 1953 to 1957, a psychology major for the last three years. At college I followed a familiar script by rebelling against my nominally Christian upbringing. (This probably happens in high school now.) I read Bertrand Russell, announced that I was an atheist, and took instant pride in my "hard-won" independence. The only disappointment was that my announcement of it was met by others with what can best be described as a yawn.

My vague, superficial Christianity had been such weak stuff that its rejection had less psychological importance than, say, breaking up with my girlfriend. In consequence, my period of active hostility to Christianity was quite brief: a few months (appropriately enough) in my sophomore year. After this began a long agnostic indifference to religion. It was a time I devoted fully to becoming a psychologist by concentrating on my graduate (1957-62) and post-graduate (1964-65) studies at Stanford University. Here I majored in the subjects of motivation and personality, which included learning and teaching the views of the self-theorists.

In graduate school, religion was treated as a pathetic anachronism. Occasionally a person's religious beliefs were "measured" in personality tests. The common interpretation was that people holding traditional religious views were fascist-authoritarian types. There was also some interest in religion on the part of social psychologists who wanted to study exotic belief systems. My contacts with the disciplines of anthropology and sociology suggested that similar attitudes were typical of people in these fields.

A year or so after I received my doctorate, my interests began to shift to experimental psychology, particularly the topics of perception, cognition, and aesthetics. This shift of interest was partly occasioned by a growing awareness that I found much humanistic personality theory intellectually confused and rather silly. Many of the arguments presented here first occurred to me in the mid-1960s. I still remember moments in

---

5. For more detailed autobiographical material see Paul C. Vitz, "A Christian Odyssey," in *Spiritual Journeys*, ed. R. Baram (Boston: St. Paul, 1987), pp. 379-99; Vitz, "My Life — So Far," in *Storying Ourselves: A Narrative Perspective on Christians in Psychology*, ed. D. J. Lee (Grand Rapids: Baker, 1993).

the middle of class lectures when I suddenly became aware that I was saying things I didn't really believe. To discover you are teaching as a reasonable approximation to scientific truth something that you no longer think is true is disconcerting, to put it mildly.

This critical suspicion continued to grow. By 1968 or so I was no longer willing to teach graduate or undergraduate courses that required me to cover the self-theorists. There things might have remained except for two unexpected events. One was the development of a nationwide mass enthusiasm for the humanistic self-theories at about the same time that I was moving away from them. The other was my conversion to Christianity. There is nothing dramatic to report about the latter — no sudden rebirth or other mystical experience — just a great deal of intense emotional turbulence associated with the collapse of my secular ideals accompanied by a quietly growing change of heart and mind. This process seems to have started sometime in 1972, and at some point since then I discovered I was a Christian — a very poor one to be sure, but still my life had been turned around. The noteworthy aspect about this is that it happened to a totally unprepared, recalcitrant, secularized psychologist who thought that the only natural direction of change was exactly in the opposite direction. There were certainly no available models for it in psychology. Becoming a Christian provided me with a dramatically different view of psychology as well as a strong motivation for developing some of the critical analysis I had begun several years earlier.

This is where things stood — with regard to my "biography" — when I first wrote this book more than fifteen years ago. Its publication contributed to many important changes in my life that have happened since. Most importantly, it put me in contact with a small but highly significant number of Christians, some of whom were psychologists, and others in different disciplines, who were also struggling with many of the problems that preoccupied me. Their response and support have been deeply appreciated and have done much to keep me in contact with a rich and increasingly innovative Christian intellectual community. The fact that I became a Catholic in 1979 has broadened my intellectual contacts still further. And much to my eternal gratitude, my Catholicism has not interfered with my friendship and sense of alliance with many Protestants, especially evangelicals. We are all in the same struggle, and we know it.

One other major change since the first edition has been my recent attempts to develop a type of positive "Christian psychology." This includes work on a narrative model of counseling; my book on Sigmund Freud, with Jesus as the anti-Oedipus; and the use of psychoanalytic concepts to support the notion of original sin.[6] Although I do think that important aspects of psychology can be effectively baptized, it is still difficult to distinguish what can be safely incorporated from what cannot. The problem is complicated still further by strong secular attacks on the basic legitimacy of psychology both as a therapeutic and as an explanatory discipline. In addition, recent decades have seen an enormous increase in the biological understanding and control of behavior, while on the other hand New Age spirituality has made it clear to many who would not listen to a Christian critique that secular psychology's interpretation of religion, and dismissal of the spiritual life, was grossly mistaken. Psychology has been losing much intellectual ground both to biology and to spirituality over the last twenty years or so. In short, psychology is no longer a young "science"; it is now a mature discipline, and it is becoming less self-confident and imperialistic than it was not so long ago.

Nevertheless, the hostility of most psychologists to Christianity is still very real. For years I was part of that sentiment; today it continues to surround me. It is a curious hostility, for psychologists are rarely consciously aware of it. Their lack of awareness is due mostly to sheer ignorance of what Christianity is — for that matter, of what any religion is. The universities are so deeply secularized that most academics can no longer articulate why they are opposed to Christianity. They merely assume that for all rational people the question of being a Christian was settled — negatively — at some time in the past.

There is one interesting difference in this hostility that has arisen since the mid-1970s. In the years since then, it has become obvious that, throughout the world, religion is alive and well. The energy of Islam is perhaps the clearest example. But the importance of Catholicism for Poland and of Eastern Orthodoxy for the fall of Soviet Communism are

---

6. Paul C. Vitz, "Narrative and Counseling, Part 1: From Analysis of the Past to Stories about It," *Journal of Psychology and Theology* 20 (1992): 11-19; Vitz, "Narrative and Counseling, Part 2: From Stories of the Past to Stories for the Future," *Journal of Psychology and Theology* 20 (1992): 20-27; Vitz, *Sigmund Freud's Christian Unconscious* (New York: Guilford Press, 1988; Grand Rapids: Eerdmans, 1993); Vitz, "A Christian Theory of Personality," in *Man and Mind,* ed. T. Burke (Hillsdale, MI: Hillsdale College Press, 1987), pp. 199-222.

commonly recognized. In the United States, the so-called Religious Right and the abortion issue have made it obvious that Christianity is not some secularized, totally irrelevant religion. In Israel and around the world, Orthodox Judaism and Hasidic life show remarkable vigor. Meanwhile, liberal Christianity and liberal Judaism both continue to decay. And what about that important political "religion," Socialism? Well, it has simply collapsed. Academics isolated from religious reality in their secular towers today look at religion with more anxiety and less smug indifference than they did in 1977. But the hostility and ignorance remain.

*   *   *

Finally, it is important to identify certain psychologies that will be explicitly excluded from our discussion. First, experimental psychology — the study of sensation, perception, cognition, memory, problem solving, and related questions — is not included. This kind of psychology, primarily found in universities and research centers, is a branch of natural science composed of various amounts of biology, physics, mathematics, and so forth. Second, the theory or philosophy of psychology known as behaviorism (the best-known example is probably that of B. F. Skinner) is not treated here, since it has little in common with humanistic self-psychology, and criticism of it would carry our discussion quite far afield. There already has been criticism of behaviorism, to which I have little to add.[7] Similarly, the therapeutic offspring of behaviorism known as behavior modification is excluded, since its techniques and principles are part of experimental psychology and its philosophy part of behaviorism.

A third omission is psychoanalysis, since much of self-psychology is a reaction against the more complex, unconscious, "pessimistic," conservative, and disciplined Freudian theories and methods. To criticize psychoanalysis with any thoroughness would require technical discussion of much material that is unrelated to the self. This would lengthen the present discussion greatly and blur its major focus.

When I first wrote this book, I did not include transpersonal psychology, since it was very new and it was hard to know what it might

7. For example, see Rodger K. Bufford, *The Human Reflex: Behavioral Psychology in Biblical Perspective* (San Francisco: Harper & Row, 1981).

become. But in this revised and expanded edition, I have devoted Chapter 9 to a critique of transpersonal psychology and to New Age spirituality, focusing on their psychological premises.

One final group is excluded, namely, those psychologists who recognize, respect, and respond to genuine religious issues in the lives of their patients. This group is not large, nor is it easily categorized. It includes psychologists who are personally committed to a religion, who integrate their faith, when appropriate, into therapy. But it also includes secular psychologists whose insights lead them to reject the contemporary religion of psychology as a superficial substitute for something genuine and a corruption of the important but limited function of psychotherapy. It is this group of psychologists who provide a basis for the hope that a strong, honest partnership may eventually develop between psychology and religion.

In spite of these exclusions, a large amount of modern psychology remains. In fact, most psychologists practicing today have been strongly affected by humanistic self-theories. Many American psychoanalysts have accepted so much of self-psychology that it is difficult to identify them as Freudian at all. Likewise, behavior modification therapists frequently espouse various self-actualizing or self-esteem philosophies in their own lives and as part of their professional ethic. Educational psychology has long been saturated with concepts like "self-esteem" and "self-actualization." In short, America's eclectic tradition has meant that almost every form of psychology today comes with a large dose of the theories criticized here.

1. Major Theorists

I shall begin by documenting the strong religious nature of much of today's psychology. This chapter presents, in brief form, the relevant theoretical positions of Carl Jung — the originator of much self-psychology — and then the positions of more recent self-theorists: Erich Fromm, Carl Rogers, Abraham Maslow, and Rollo May (May being important primarily as a representative of existential psychology). The popularization of these and other self-theorists will be described briefly and critiqued in the next chapter. More detailed criticisms of the common assumptions of the self-theory position will be taken up in later chapters.

Jung, Fromm, Rogers, Maslow, and May have been selected as the most influential self-theorists. Other psychologists have contributed to self-theory, but in general they have not been as completely committed to the concept of the self. The psychoanalytic ego-psychologists, for example, with their notions of the conflict-free ego sphere and ego mechanisms of defense, which were developed in the 1930s and 1940s by Heinz Hartmann and Anna Freud and others, are not pure self-psychologists, since they remained committed to much of traditional Freudian theory.[1] Emphasis on the self is present but is not very strong in the works of famous earlier deviants from orthodox Freudianism such as Rank, Adler, and Horney. Nevertheless, to the extent that these theorists whom we have omitted do emphasize the self (for example, Adler with his notion of the creative self, and Horney with her concern

---

1. See Heinz Hartmann, "Psychoanalysis and the Concept of Health," *International Journal of Psychoanalysis* 20 (1939): 308-21; Anna Freud, *The Ego and the Mechanisms of Defense* (London: Hogarth, 1942); Ernst Kris, "Ego Psychology and Interpretation in Psychoanalytic Therapy," *Psychoanalytic Quarterly* 20 (1951).

for self-realization), their ideas and impact are similar to those we present below.[2]

CARL JUNG

Jung was born in Switzerland in 1875. His father was a pastor in the Swiss Reformed Church, and he rebelled against his father and his father's religion. Jung obtained a medical degree in 1900 and then specialized in psychiatry. A short time later he met Sigmund Freud, and they had a few years of collaboration, followed by a serious and permanent break. Jung was critical of Freud's extreme emphasis on sexuality; he was also much less interested in psychopathology and more concerned with people's spiritual needs.

Indeed, Jung was quite aware of the religious nature of psychotherapy, and the theological cast of much of his writing is apparent. For example, *An Answer to Job*[3] is an extensive, but heterodox, exercise in scriptural interpretation. Jung's explicit awareness of the religious issue is stated when he writes: "Patients force the psychotherapist into the role of priest, and expect and demand that he shall free them from distress. That is why we psychotherapists must occupy ourselves with problems which strictly speaking belong to the Theologian."[4]

Jung's psychology — unlike Freud's — provided positive, synthetic concepts that could serve as a conscious goal not only for therapy but also for life as a whole. Jung responded far more to the patient's demand for general relief from distress than did Freud.[5] Jung's positive answer

2. For examples of these theorists' emphasis on the self, see A. Adler, "The Fundamental Views of Individual Psychology," *International Journal of Individual Psychology* 1 (1935): 5-8; K. Horney, *Neurosis and Human Growth: The Struggle toward Self-realization* (New York: Norton, 1950).

3. Carl Jung, *An Answer to Job*, trans. R. F. C. Hull (London: Routledge and Kegan Paul, 1954).

4. Carl Jung, *Modern Man in Search of a Soul* (New York: Harcourt, Brace, 1933), p. 278.

5. Freud was quite aware of the religious character of Jungian and Adlerian psychology, whence derives much of the psychology used in selfism. Freud made a sharp distinction between religion and psychoanalysis, and he claimed that analysts "cannot guide patients in their synthesis; we can by analytic work only prepare them for it." And he declared: "We do not seek to bring him [the patient] relief by receiving him into the catholic, protestant or socialist community." Freud saw the Adlerians as "buffoons . . .'.

to the patient's basic religious needs is summarized by Jacobi, a prominent student of his:

> Jungian psychotherapy is . . . a *Heilsweg,* in the twofold sense of the
> German word: a way of healing and a way of salvation. It has the power
> to cure. . . . in addition it knows the way and has the means to lead the
> individual to his 'salvation,' to the knowledge and fulfillment of his
> personality, which have always been the aim of spiritual striving. Jung's
> system of thought can be explained theoretically only up to a certain
> point; to understand it fully one must have experienced or, better still,
> 'suffered' its living action in oneself. Apart from its medical aspect,
> Jungian psychotherapy is thus a system of education and spiritual
> guidance.[6]

The process of Jungian movement on this path is, Jacobi continues,
"both ethically and intellectually an extremely difficult task, which can
be successfully performed only by the fortunate few, those elected and
favored by grace."[7] The last stage, really a process, on the Jungian path
of individuation is called self-realization. This goal of self-realization or
self-actualization is at heart a gnostic one, in which the commandment
"Know and express thyself" has replaced the Judeo-Christian commandment "Love God and others." (In many respects, all modern psychology
of whatever theoretical persuasion, because of the emphasis on special,
somewhat esoteric knowledge, can be interpreted as part of a vast gnostic
heresy.)[8]

Very briefly, this process of self-realization involves (1) the patient's
discovery and understanding of the archetypes (i.e., structures and
desires) in his or her collective and personal unconscious and (2) the
interpretation and expression of these archetypes in the patient's life. In

---

who published books about the meaning of life[!]." Ernest Kris, "Some Vicissitudes of
Insight in Psychoanalysis," *International Journal of Psychoanalysis* 37 (Nov.-Dec. 1956): 453;
Sigmund Freud, *The Question of Lay Analysis* (New York: Norton, 1950), p. 256; Ernest L.
Freud, ed., *Letters of Sigmund Freud* (New York: Basic Books, 1960), p. 401.

    6. J. Jacobi, *The Psychology of C. G. Jung,* 8th ed. (New Haven: Yale University Press,
1973), p. 60.

    7. Jacobi, *Psychology of C. G. Jung,* p. 127.

    8. For the basic gnostic character (i.e., emphasizing knowledge as salvation) of
modernism, including psychology, see, e.g., Eric Voegelin, *Science, Politics and Gnosticism*
(Chicago: Regnery, 1968). For the gnostic character of transpersonal psychology, see
below, Chapter 9.

any case, the Jungian model simply assumes that the goal of life is self-realization. As a goal or purpose of life, self-actualization cannot be scientifically justified; it is based on unexamined philosophical and moral assumptions.

Much Jungian psychology is not explicitly focused on individuation (self-realization) but is concerned with the symbolic interpretation of the patient's dreams, writings, drawings, etc. Here Jung's analysis is focused on the collective and personal unconscious of the patient and on archetypes and other concepts. Jung acknowledges the patient's basic religious concerns, and Jungian psychology is directly applied to the expression of the patient's archetypal religious motives — for example, in dreams about the wise old man (a God archetype), dreams about rebirth, and so on. Jung's discovery of the psychology of religious symbols is important, but there is with all this focusing on one's inner life a real danger of substituting the psychological experience of one's religious unconscious for genuine religious experience that comes through a transcendent God who acts in history. Those who make this mistake have truly treated psychology as religion.[9]

ERICH FROMM

Erich Fromm was born in 1900, educated at Heidelberg, Frankfurt, and Munich, received psychoanalytic training in Berlin, and came to the United States in 1933. He lived in the United States and Mexico for much of the rest of his life. Fromm was originally a Freudian psychoanalyst, but he broke from this tradition in the 1930s. Fromm rejected Freud's emphasis on the biological nature of humankind, especially disputing Freud's inclusion of aggression (the death instinct) as a basic part of human nature. Freud gave aggression the same importance as sex (the life instinct), while Fromm, in contrast, emphasized society as the major determinant of human personality. In particular, Fromm described human nature as intrinsically and naturally good and attributed anything bad — evil — to society, especially when society causes the self to deny

---

9. See R. Hostie, *Religion and the Psychology of Jung,* trans. G. R. Lamb (New York: Sheed and Ward, 1957). For a detailed discussion of Jung's religious assumptions, etc., see D. S. Browning, *Religious Thought and the Modern Psychologies* (Philadelphia: Fortress Press, 1987).

its own potential for growth and expression. Except for the unconscious influence of society, Fromm came to neglect the traditional psychoanalytic theory of the unconscious — for instance, dreams.

In spite of his break with the Freudian tradition, Fromm remained deeply influenced by Freud, often citing or criticizing him. He shared Freud's penchant for characterizing cultural belief systems and those who believe them in terms of psychological types, such as the "exploitative" and "marketing" character types of capitalist society or the "authoritative" and "regressive" beliefs characterizing the Christian doctrine of the Trinity.[10] The following remarks are typical of Fromm:

> A spirit of pride and optimism has distinguished Western culture in the last few centuries. . . . Man's pride has been justified. By virtue of his reason he has built a material world the reality of which surpasses even the dreams and visions of fairy tales and utopias. He harnesses physical energies which will enable the human race to secure the material conditions necessary for a dignified and productive existence, and although many of his goals have not yet been attained there is hardly any doubt that they are within reach and that *the problem of production* — which was the problem in the past — is, in principle, solved.[11]

Elsewhere in the same book he speaks in the same optimistic vein of human character:

> I shall attempt to show that the character structure of the mature and integrated personality, the productive character, constitutes the source and basis of "virtue," and that "vice," in the last analysis, is indifference to one's own self and self-mutilation. Not self-renunciation nor selfishness but the affirmation of his truly human self, are the supreme values of humanistic ethics. If man is to have confidence in values, he must know himself and the capacity of his nature for goodness and productiveness.[12]

10. See E. Fromm, *Escape from Freedom* (New York: Holt, Rinehart & Winston, 1941); Fromm, *The Dogma of Christ and Other Essays* (New York: Holt, Rinehart & Winston, 1955). Also relevant are Fromm's *You Shall Be as Gods* (New York: Holt, Rinehart & Winston, 1966) and *The Sane Society* (New York: Rinehart, 1955).

11. Erich Fromm, *Man for Himself* (New York: Rinehart, 1947); quoted from the Fawcett Premier Book edition (Greenwich, CT: Fawcett, n.d.), pp. 13-14; italics in original.

12. Fromm, *Man for Himself*, p. 17.

In this view, a value such as love for one's neighbor is not viewed as a phenomenon transcending man;

> it is something inherent and *radiating from* him. Love is not a higher power which descends upon man nor a duty which is imposed upon him; it is his own power by which he relates himself to the world and makes it truly his.[13]

This of course has consequences for one's idea of what human nature is in itself:

> The position taken by humanistic ethics that man is able to know what is good and to act accordingly on the strength of his natural potentialities and of his reason would be untenable if the dogma of man's innate natural evilness were true.[14]

Fromm's hostility to Christianity is clear in *The Dogma of Christ,* where he argues that belief in God always functions as "the ally of the rulers."[15] (This is a position he must have found difficult to reconcile with the persecution of Christian believers by atheistic rulers in, say, the Soviet Union, Albania, or China; and after the fall of Communism in Eastern Europe and the Soviet Union, his claim looks simply stupid.) Fromm claims that Christianity arose from a proletariat class so frustrated in its hopes for political and social change that it turned to salvation in a fantasy world of the supernatural.[16] His own religious position is quite explicit in *You Shall Be as Gods:* the concept of god has evolved to the point that humankind is God, and if the sacred exists, its center is in the self and the selves of others. Fromm's ideal society is humanistic, communitarian socialism, which he presents in considerable detail in *The Sane Society* (1955).

Throughout Fromm's works, his atheism and materialism, his political views, and other values so permeate his psychology that it is hard even to identify those contributions which might reasonably be considered scientific.

---

13. Fromm, *Man for Himself,* p. 23; italics in original.
14. Fromm, *Man for Himself,* p. 212.
15. Fromm, *Dogma of Christ,* p. 15.
16. Fromm, *Dogma of Christ,* section III, e.g., p. 35.

CARL ROGERS

Carl Rogers, a Midwestern American, was born in 1902. He describes himself as "the middle child in a large, close-knit family where hard work and a highly conservative Protestant Christianity were about equally revered."[17] He was graduated in 1924 from the University of Wisconsin, having switched from agricultural science to preparation for the ministry. He attended Union Theological Seminary in New York City, where he was exposed to a liberal philosophical viewpoint regarding religion. After a short visit abroad he broke from Christianity, deciding that he wanted to help humanity without being inhibited by any prior commitment to a fixed set of beliefs whose truth was not obvious to him. He transferred to the Teachers College at Columbia University, where he was influenced by John Dewey's thought, and received the Ph.D. degree in 1928.

From Rogers's varied exposure to different psychological theories he developed his own position, which has become highly influential. We shall omit discussion of his technique of therapy called "non-directive," or "client-centered," and concentrate on his theory of personality and the goals of therapy. The central work for our purposes is *On Becoming a Person*. Here Rogers states the goal of therapy as follows:

> If I can create a relationship characterized on my part: by a genuineness and transparency, *in which I am my real feelings; by a warm acceptance of and prizing of the other person as a separate individual;* by a sensitive ability to see his world and himself as he sees them; then the other individual in the relationship: will experience and understand aspects of himself which previously he has repressed; will find *himself becoming better integrated*, more able to function effectively; will become more similar to the person he would like to be; will be *more self-directing and more self-confident;* will become *more of a person, more unique and more self-expressive;* will be more understanding, more acceptant of others; will be able to cope with the problems of life more adequately and more comfortably.
>
> I believe this statement holds whether I am speaking of my relationship with a client, with a group of students or staff members, with my family or children. It seems to me that *we have here a general hypothesis*

17. Quoted in Calvin S. Hall and Gardner Lindzey, *Introduction to Theories of Personality* (New York: Wiley, 1985), chaps. 4 and 6; this book is the source of biographical information provided here about Rogers, Fromm, and Maslow.

which offers exciting possibilities for the development of creative, adaptive, autonomous persons.[18]

Psychotherapy, once a restricted and specialized activity, is now generalized to all of life's relations. Rogers's writings are much more oriented toward the process of therapy than Fromm's, and he tends to ignore large cultural and historical themes. He interprets therapy as a process of the changing and growing self:

> I shall assume that the *client experiences himself as being fully received.* By this I mean that whatever his feelings — fear, despair, insecurity, anger; whatever his mode of expression — silence, gestures, tears, or words; whatever he finds himself being in this moment, *he senses that he is psychologically received, just as he is, by the therapist.*[19]

More explicitly, Rogers describes his theory of therapy as follows:

> Individuals move, I began to see, not from a fixity or homeostasis through change to a new fixity, though such a process is indeed possible. But much the more significant continuum is from fixity to changingness, from rigid structure to flow, from stasis to process.[20]

At the first stage of the therapeutic process, the person is fixed, static, completely blocked; he is either unaware of his feelings and emotions or attributes them to objective external circumstances. By the second or third stage (out of seven), we have people described as follows:

> "And yet there is the matter of, well, how much do you leave yourself open to marriage, and if your professional vocation is important, and that's the one thing that's really yourself at this point, it does place a limitation on your contact."
>
> In this excerpt the self is such a remote object that this would probably best be classified as being between stages two and three.
>
> *There is also expression about the self as a reflected object, existing primarily in others.*
>
> *There is much expression about or description of feelings and personal meanings not now present.*

18. Carl R. Rogers, *On Becoming a Person* (Boston: Houghton Mifflin, 1961), pp. 37-38; italics added.
19. Rogers, *On Becoming a Person*, p. 130; italics added.
20. Rogers, *On Becoming a Person*, p. 131.

There is very little acceptance of feelings. For the most part feelings are revealed as something shameful, bad, or abnormal, or unacceptable in other ways.[21]

The fifth stage Rogers describes as follows:

Feelings are expressed freely as in the present.
"I expect kinda to get a severe rejection — this I expect all the time . . . somehow I guess I even feel it with you. . . . It's hard to talk about because I want to be the best I can possibly be with you."
Feelings are very close to being fully experienced. They "bubble up," "seep through," in spite of the fear and distrust which the client feels at experiencing them with fullness and immediacy.
"That kinda came out and I just don't understand it. *(Long pause)* I'm trying to get hold of what that terror is."
Client is talking about an external event. Suddenly she gets a pained, stricken look.
Therapist: "What — what's hitting you now?"
Client: "I don't know. *(She cries)* . . . I must have been getting a little too close to something I didn't want to talk about, or something."[22]

The culmination of Rogerian therapy is the seventh and highest stage, which is summarized as follows:

The process moves from a point of fixity, where all the elements and threads described are separately discernible and separately understandable, to the flowing peak moments of therapy in which all these threads become inseparably woven together. In the new experiencing with immediacy which occurs at such moments, feeling and cognition interpenetrate, self is subjectively present in the experience, volition is simply the subjective following of a harmonious balance of organismic direction. . . . [T]he person becomes a unity of flow, or motion. . . . [H]e has become an integrated process of changingness.[23]

---

21. Rogers, *On Becoming a Person*, pp. 135-36; italics in original.
22. Rogers, *On Becoming a Person*, pp. 139-40; italics in original.
23. Rogers, *On Becoming a Person*, p. 158.

ABRAHAM MASLOW

Abraham Maslow was born in 1908 and grew up in Brooklyn. He was primarily educated at the University of Wisconsin. He then spent his early professional years in New York City at Columbia Teachers College and Brooklyn College. His independently developed theory of the self is close to Rogers's, but his distinctive concepts deserve mention.

Maslow postulates a hierarchy of human needs. This hierarchy, whose basis is assumed to be innate, requires that needs must be satisfied in a relatively fixed order, starting with basic physiological and safety needs, proceeding to needs for belonging and love, for self-esteem and status, and finally reaching the highest need, the need for self-realization, or self-actualization, as Maslow calls it. This last need is the most distinctively human, although it depends for fulfillment on the prior satisfaction of the lower needs. The person in whom this final need is satisfied is the self-actualized person, an ideal type with the following distinctive characteristics:

(1) efficient perception of reality and comfortableness with it;
(2) acceptance of self and others;
(3) spontaneity;
(4) an autonomous self independent of culture; '
(5) creativity (a universal hallmark of the ideal person among self-theorists);
(6) having "peak" experiences, that is, oceanic or mystic experiences (a peak experience is, however, a natural phenomenon, not a supernatural one, according to Maslow);
(7) democratic, egalitarian, and humanitarian character structure and values.[24]

Maslow's description of the essential quality of these self-actualized types is revealing:

A few centuries ago these would all have been described as men who walk in the path of God or as godly men. A few say that they believe in God, but describe this God more as a metaphysical concept than as

24. Abraham Maslow, *Motivation and Personality*, 2d ed. (New York: Harper, 1970), chap. 11.

a personal figure. If religion is defined only in social-behavioral terms, then these are all religious people, the atheist included. But if more conservatively we use the term religion so as to include and stress the supernatural element and institutional orthodoxy (certainly the more common usage) then our answer must be quite different, for then almost none of them is religious.

[Creativeness] is a universal characteristic of all the people studied or observed. There is no exception. Each one shows in one way or another a special kind of creativeness or originality or inventiveness that has certain peculiar characteristics. . . . For one thing, it is different from the special creativeness of the Mozart type. We may as well face the fact that so-called geniuses display ability that we do not understand. . . . Such talent we have no concern with here since it does not rest upon psychic health or basic satisfaction. The creativeness of the self-actualized man seems rather to be kin to the naive and universal creativeness of unspoiled children.[25]

Maslow names some of these secular saints — Lincoln in his last days, Thomas Jefferson, Einstein, Eleanor Roosevelt, Jane Addams, William James, Spinoza, and aspects of Walt Whitman, Thoreau, Beethoven, George Washington Carver, Goethe, Eugene V. Debs, Albert Schweitzer, and so on.[26]

ROLLO MAY AND EXISTENTIAL PSYCHOLOGY

Our last theorist is Rollo May, who is important for us because he exemplifies the influence of existential philosophy on American self-psychology. Born in 1909, he received the Bachelor of Arts degree from Oberlin, a Bachelor of Divinity from Union Theological Seminary, and the Ph.D. at Columbia Teachers College. (Thus his educational background is remarkably similar to that of Rogers and Maslow: all moved from states in the Great Lakes area to New York City and Columbia Teachers College — and in two cases attended Union Seminary across the street.) May's special contribution to self-theory comes from the European influence of existentialism, which he first encountered in his psychotherapeutic studies in Vienna.

25. Maslow, *Motivation and Personality*, pp. 169-70.
26. Maslow, *Motivation and Personality*, p. 152.

Existentialism as a philosophy is notoriously hard to characterize rigorously, and existential therapy has the same difficulty. It is, however, possible to isolate some special themes in existential therapy that represent a distinctive strand in the framework of self-theory.

The central concept is probably that of "being there" *(Dasein)*, by which is meant the intense fundamental awareness of one's existence. This basic experience is described by a patient of May's, a young woman who reported:

> Then what is left? What is left is this, "I am." This act of contact and acceptance with "I am," once gotten hold of, gave me (what I think was for me the first time) the experience since I am, I have the right to be.
>   What is this experience like? . . . It is the experience of my own aliveness. . . . It is my saying to Descartes, "I AM, therefore, I think, I feel, I do."[27]

This "I am" experience is the basic experience of being, and although it is not itself a solution to a patient's problem, May claims that it is a necessary precondition for successful analysis.

One important property of being is that it rejects the distinction between the knowing or experiencing subject and the known or experienced object. Instead, the concept of being is a basic part of the existentialist "endeavor to understand man by cutting below the cleavage between subject and object which has bedeviled Western thought and science since shortly after the Renaissance."[28] This condition of being is inseparable from its opposite — the condition of nonbeing or nothingness. Awareness of and confrontation with nonbeing, especially in the form of death, gives rise to the powerful and pervasive emotion of angst (dread or anxiety). Therefore, at the very center of existentialist thought is the common modern condition of pervasive anxiety that is "the experience of the threat of imminent non-being."[29]

This existence takes place in a world or universe characterized as "Being-in-the-world." The three aspects of the existential world are the *Umwelt* (the "world around," the environment), the *Mitwelt* (the "world with" others, our life of social and interpersonal relations), and, most central, the *Eigenwelt* (the "own world," the world of the self and rela-

27. Rollo May, *Existence* (New York: Basic Books, 1958), p. 43.
28. May, *Existence,* p. 11.
29. May, *Existence,* p. 50.

tionship to one's self). Two or all three of these worlds may be experienced at the same time, but taken together they are the only arenas within which our existence takes place.

An important existential concept is "becoming," the process of self-development or fulfilling one's potential. This process unfolds by way of the self's choosing its own course of self-fulfillment. Acts of choice bring the self from initial existence into an actualized self, with a nature or essence created by its choice. Thus, the self first exists (i.e., "I am"), but without any a priori nature or essence. Instead, through acts of choice the self's essence is created. These choices are courageously made in the face of the self's awareness of nonbeing and its experience of angst. Guilt arises through failure to develop the self's potential, through blocking or ignoring one's chance to become one's potential. Transcendence is the name of the important capacity of the existential self to surpass or climb beyond the prior level of self-development. Thus, as self-potential is developed, each new stage is a transcending of the earlier stages; this process often is called "becoming."

Rollo May points out that Carl Rogers, although he never had direct contact with existentialism, developed a therapy with important existential aspects, especially in Rogers's emphases on becoming and on the therapist's direct experience of himself and of the patient.

> I launch myself into the therapeutic relationship having a hypothesis, or a faith, that my liking, my confidence, and my understanding of the other person's inner world, will lead to a significant process of becoming. I enter the relationship not as a scientist, not as a physician who can accurately diagnose and cure, but as a person, entering into a personal relationship. Insofar as I see him only as an object, the client will tend to become only an object.[30]

A final significant point is the claim of existential psychology that a natural science of human beings is not possible. Jean-Paul Sartre expresses this as a refusal "to consider man as capable of being analyzed and reduced to original givens, to determined desires (or drives), supported by the subject as properties [are] by an object."[31]

---

30. May, *Existence*, p. 82; quoting from Carl Rogers, "Persons or Science? A Philosophical Question," *American Psychologist* 10 (1955): 267-78.

31. Jean-Paul Sartre, *Being and Nothingness*, trans. Hazel E. Barnes (New York: Philosophical Library, 1956), p. 561.

In summary, existential therapy — like existential philosophy — starts with the isolated self, aware of its basic existence, but confronted by nonexistence and the associated emotion of dread. This self, valued and accepted directly by the therapist, is encouraged, in the face of nonbeing, courageously to develop self-defined decisions that will bring its potential to fulfillment. This transcendent activity, or becoming-through-choosing, also creates the essence of the individual. On the other hand, failure to fulfill self-potential causes guilt. When this process succeeds, an individual who initially had only an existence has now created his or her own essence.

This self-knowledge is arrived at by the patient's learning the meaning of his or her experienced states on their own terms, that is, phenomenologically and not via some "objective" subject-object philosophy, as found in natural science. All of this takes place in a universe that excludes God and is limited to three aspects: the external environment, the social and interpersonal environment, and the self and its relation to itself.

2. Self-Theory for Everybody

Jung, Fromm, Rogers, Maslow, and May were all theoreticians. Their concepts — however influential with intellectuals and students — had to be translated into popular form before they could reach large numbers of people. Some of those who have done this job of translation have pushed the ideas of these theorists to extremes for which they should not be held responsible. Yet it should be borne in mind that the popularizers are primarily professional psychologists or psychiatrists, and their works do represent a legitimate presentation or logical extension of self-theory. Actually the line between "theorist" and "popularizer" cannot be drawn all that precisely. With the exception of Jung, none of the preceding theorists is likely to merit classification as a major thinker. At best, they introduced interesting and useful but limited concepts. At worst, they simply marketed already existing ideas like self-actualization, and a good number of their works are indistinguishable from popularization. I am thinking especially of Rogers's *Carl Rogers on Encounter Groups* and *Becoming Partners: Marriage and Its Alternatives,* both of which are discussed below.

Keep in mind that many of the particular expressions of self-theory, such as those we shall describe, are apt to be very short-lived. Despite their prominence a few years ago, encounter groups, for instance, seem to have all but disappeared. But new forms of popularized self-theory continually arise — for example, today's great concern with self-esteem.

SELF-ESTEEM

Historically speaking, the concept of self-esteem has no clear intellectual origins; no major theorist has made it a central concept. Many psychol-

15

ogists have emphasized the self, in various ways, but the usual focus has been on self-actualization, fulfillment of one's full potential. As a result, it is hard to trace the direct source of this emphasis on self-esteem. Apparently, this widespread preoccupation is a distillation of the general concern with the self found in so many psychological theories. Self-esteem seems to be a common denominator pervading the writings of such varied theorists as Carl Rogers, Abraham Maslow, "ego-strength" psychologists, and various recent moral educators. In any case, the concern with self-esteem hovers everywhere in America today. It is, however, most reliably found in the world of education — from professors of education to principals, teachers, school boards, and television programs concerned with preschool-age children.[1]

The basic idea of self-esteem in American education is that students should be told how wonderful and important they are by teachers and through exercises in the curriculum that have the students (or teachers) saying or writing all kinds of positive things about themselves.[2] This is often called "self-talk." In California, a task force was established to introduce self-esteem education into the curriculum at all grade levels and in many different subject materials. Those who worked on and developed this California material believed that low self-esteem was a major cause of everything from drug use to teenage pregnancy to low reading and math scores to discipline problems and high drop out rates. Proposals to raise self-esteem involved giving rewards, prizes, etc., to all students regardless of performance. Self-esteem was not linked to performance since this would raise the possibility of failure, or inadequate performance, which would (according to the theory) perpetuate low self-esteem.

What is wrong with the concept of self-esteem? Lots — and it is fundamental in nature. There have been thousands of psychological studies on self-esteem. The bottom line is that self-esteem is a complex notion, defined and measured in many different and ambiguous ways (e.g., self-image, self-worth, ego-strength, etc.). And whatever self-esteem is taken to mean, no reliable evidence supports the utility of self-esteem

---

1. See "The Curse of Self-Esteem," *Newsweek*, 17 Feb. 1992; see also *U.S. News and World Report*, 1 April 1990, p. 16.

2. See Rita Kramer, *Ed School Follies: The Miseducation of America's Teachers* (New York: Free Press, 1991); Chester E. Finn, Jr., "Narcissus Goes to School," *Commentary* 89 (June 1990): 40-45.

scores to predict important behaviors.[3] There is no evidence that high self-esteem itself reliably causes anything — and, indeed, lots of people with little of it have achieved a great deal in one context or another. For instance, Gloria Steinem, who has written a number of books and has been a major leader of the feminist movement, recently revealed in *Revolution from Within: A Book of Self-Esteem* that she suffers from (of all things) low self-esteem.[4] By contrast, many people with high self-esteem are happy just being rich, beautiful, or socially connected. Some other people whose high self-esteem has been noted are inner-city drug dealers, who generally feel quite good about themselves; after all, they have succeeded in making a lot of money in a hostile and competitive environment.

A 1989 study of mathematical skills compared students in eight different countries.[5] American students ranked lowest in mathematical competence, and Korean students ranked highest. But the researchers also asked students to rate how good they were at mathematics. The Americans ranked highest in self-judged mathematical ability, while the Koreans ranked lowest. Mathematical self-esteem had an inverse relation to mathematical accomplishment! This is certainly an example of a "feel-good" psychology keeping students from an accurate perception of reality. The self-esteem theory predicts that only those who feel good about themselves will do well — which is supposedly why all students need self-esteem — but feeling good about yourself may simply make you overconfident, narcissistic, and unable to work hard.

I am not implying that high self-esteem is always negatively related to accomplishment. Rather, the research mentioned above shows that measures of self-esteem have no reliable relationship to behavior, either positive or negative. In part, this is simply because life is too complicated for so simple a notion to be of much use. But we should expect this failure in advance. We all know, and know of, people who are motivated by insecurities and self-doubts. These are often both the heroes and the

3. Susan Black, "Self-Esteem: Sense and Nonsense," *American School Board Journal* 178 (July 1991): 27-29; Black, "Research Says . . . ," *American School Board Journal* 179 (March 1992): 26-28.

4. Gloria Steinem, *Revolution from Within: A Book of Self-Esteem* (Boston: Little, Brown, 1992).

5. A. LaPointe, N. A. Mead, and G. Philips, *A World of Difference: An International Assessment of Mathematics and Science* (Princeton, NJ: Educational Testing Service, 1989), p. 10.

villains of history. The prevalence of certain men of small stature in the history of aggressive military leadership is well documented: Julius Caesar, Napoleon, Hitler, and Stalin were all small men determined to prove that they were "big." It is not uncommon for great athletes and others to overcome grave physical disabilities — and a lack of self-esteem. Many superior achievements appear to have their origin in what psychologist Alfred Adler called "over-compensation" in response to an "inferiority complex."

The point is not that feeling bad about ourselves is good, but rather that only two things can truly change how we feel about ourselves: producing real accomplishments and having "basic trust." Genuine accomplishment in the real world creates and justifies our attitudes. A child who learns to read, who can do mathematics, who can play the piano or baseball will have a true sense of accomplishment and an appropriate sense of self-esteem. Schools that fail to teach reading, writing, and arithmetic corrupt the proper understanding of self-esteem. Educators who say "Don't grade them, don't label them. You have to make them feel good about themselves" cause the problems.[6] It makes no sense for students to be full of self-esteem if they are empty of knowledge. Reality will soon puncture their illusions, and they will have to face two disturbing facts: (1) that they are ignorant, and (2) that the adults responsible for teaching them have both failed them and lied to them. In the real world, praise has to be the reward for something worthwhile; praise must be connected to reality.

There is an even more fundamental way in which most people come to genuine self-esteem — actually, to feelings of self-worth and what psychologists call "basic trust": through receiving love. To begin with, our mother's love. But this foundational experience of love and self-confidence cannot be faked. When teachers attempt to create this deep and important experience by pretending that they "love" all their students and by praising them indiscriminately, they misunderstand the nature of this kind of love. Parental love simply cannot be manufactured by a teacher in a few minutes of interaction a day for each of dozens of students. The child knows not only that such love is fake but also that real teachers are supposed to teach, and that this involves not just support but discipline, demands, and reprimands. The best, most admired, and

6. As quoted in Kramer, *Ed School Follies*; see also p. 210 in the chapter entitled "Self-Esteem Has Replaced Understanding as the Goal of Education."

most loved teachers in our high schools today are often the athletic coaches. They still teach, they still demand performance — and they rarely worry about self-esteem.

Similar problems arise for those who try to build their own flagging self-esteem by speaking lovingly to their insecure "inner child." Such attempts are doomed to failure for two reasons. First, if we are insecure about our self-worth, how can we believe our own praise? And second, like the child, we know the need for self-discipline and accomplishment.

Self-esteem should be understood as a response, not as a cause. It is primarily an emotional response to what we have done, and to what others have done to us. While it is a desirable feeling or internal state, like happiness it does not cause much. Also like happiness, and like love, self-esteem is almost impossible to get by trying to get it. Try to acquire self-esteem and you will fail — but do good to others and accomplish something for yourself, and you will have all the self-esteem you need.

The subject is vital for Christians, partly because so many are so concerned about it, and partly because the recovery of self-esteem has been touted as tantamount to a new reformation. We must note, however, that self-esteem is a deeply secular concept — not one with which Christians should be particularly concerned. A Christian should have a tremendous sense of self-worth: God made us in his image; he loves us; he sent his Son to save each of us; our destiny is to be with him forever. Each of us is of such value that the angels rejoice over every repentant sinner. But on the other hand, we have nothing on our own to be proud of; we were given life along with all our talents, and we are all poor sinners. There is certainly no theological reason to believe that the high in self-esteem are more favored by God and more likely to reach heaven; in fact, there is far more evidence to the contrary: "Blessed are the meek. . . ."

In addition, self-esteem is based on the very American notion that each of us is responsible for our own happiness. Thus, within a Christian framework, self-esteem has a subtle, pathological aspect: many take the "pursuit of happiness" as a far more intense personal goal than the pursuit of holiness. Today, self-esteem is thought to be essential to happiness: unless you love yourself, you will not be happy. But to assume that we must love ourselves, that God will not love us as much as we need to be loved, is a form of practical atheism. We say we believe in God — but we don't trust him. Instead, many Christians live by the very unbiblical motto "God loves those who love themselves."

Another problem is that Americans have begun to excuse evil or destructive behavior on the grounds of "low self-esteem." But self-esteem, whether high or low, does not determine our actions. We are accountable for our actions, and we are responsible for trying to do good and avoid evil. Low self-esteem does not make someone an alcoholic, nor does it enable a person finally to admit his or her addiction and do something about it. Both of these decisions are up to each of us, whatever our level of self-esteem.

THE SELF-SERVING BIAS

Although many people seem to think that their problem or the problem of others is their lack of self-esteem, or a lack of a sufficiently positive attitude toward themselves, there is much psychological evidence to the contrary. Many experiments in social psychology have shown that people have a reliable tendency to interpret events as favorable to them, even when the facts don't justify this. This well-documented tendency is called the "self-serving bias."[7] For example, in experiments where people are allowed to succeed or to fail, independent of their own actions, subjects reliably attribute success to their own efforts and failure to things other than themselves. For instance, failure might be due to bad luck, to the intrinsic difficulty of the task, or to the mediocre or incompetent partner they had in the experiment. In short, human beings are very prone to take responsibility for success and to blame others or circumstances for failure. Related to this is the fact that most people see themselves as "above average" in most important respects.

It was once proposed that mental health meant that a person was in close touch with reality, that a person had an objective and realistic

7. See G. W. Bradley, "Self-serving Biases in the Attribution Process: A Reexamination of the Fact or Fiction Question," *Journal of Personality and Social Psychology* 36 (1978): 56-71; D. T. Miller and M. Ross, "Self-serving Biases in the Attribution of Causality: Fact or Fiction?" *Psychological Bulletin* 82 (1975): 213-25; D. T. Miller and C. A. Porter (1988), "Errors and Biases in the Attribution Process," in *Social-Personal Inference in Clinical Psychology,* ed. L. Abramson (New York: Guilford, 1988), pp. 3-29; M. Zuckerman, "Attribution of Success and Failure Revisited, or: The Motivational Bias Is Alive and Well in Attribution Theory," *Journal of Personality* 47 (1979): 256-87. For a theoretical discussion, see David G. Myers, *The Inflated Self: Human Illusions and the Biblical Call to Hope* (New York: Seabury, 1981).

knowledge of his or her strengths and weaknesses. But it is now clear that the great majority of us are so reliably biased in favor of our own capacities and prospects that it is hard to find people who are truly realistic about themselves. Another example of this bias is the tendency for people to trust their own judgments in many situations in which it can be shown that objectively they have little basis for confidence. In any case, it looks like human beings are reliably biased in favor of themselves in many different situations, and there is little reason to believe that even those who are supposedly lacking in self-esteem are also lacking in a self-serving bias.

Finally, the whole focus on our selves feeds unrealistic self-love, which psychologists often call "narcissism." One would have thought America had enough trouble with the narcissism of the "Me Generation" in the 1970s and with the Yuppies in the 1980s. But today's search for self-esteem is just the newest expression of America's tradition of ego-mania. And giving schoolchildren happy faces on all their homework just because it was handed in, or giving them trophies for just being on the team, is flattery of the kind found for decades in our commercial slogans. Such self-preoccupation is an extreme expression of an individualistic psychology first created by a frontier society and now supported and corrupted by consumerism. Today it is reinforced by educators who gratify the vanity of even our youngest children with repetitive mantras like: "The most important person in the whole wide world is you, and you hardly even know you!"[8] The "feel good" created by such words is an illusion and is closer to a drug-induced high than to any reality. It pacifies, seduces, distracts. It fills the empty self, but it perpetuates passivity and weakness.

This narcissistic emphasis in our society, and especially in education, is a thinly disguised form of self-worship. If accepted, America would have 250 million "most important persons in the whole wide world" — 250 million golden selves. If such idolatry were not socially so dangerous, it would be funny; instead, it is truly pathetic.

---

8. This well-known refrain comes from *Sesame Street*, the extremely popular children's TV program.

ENCOUNTER GROUPS

An important, special environment for spreading self-theory has been the small group generally known as an encounter group. According to Rogers, these groups, which come in many varieties — among them T-groups, Gestalt therapy, and creativity workshops — have the following common characteristics:

> A facilitator can develop, in a group which meets intensively, a psychological climate of safety in which freedom of expression and reduction of defensiveness gradually occur.
>
> A climate of mutual trust develops out of this mutual freedom to express real feelings, positive and negative. Each member moves toward greater acceptance of his total being — emotional, intellectual and physical — as it is, including its potential.
>
> With individuals less inhibited by defensive rigidity, the possibility of change in personal attitudes and behavior . . . becomes less threatening.
>
> There is a development of feedback from one person to another, such that each individual learns how he appears to others and what impact he has in interpersonal relationships.
>
> With this greater freedom and improved communication, new ideas, new concepts, new directions emerge. Innovation can become a desirable rather than a threatening possibility.
>
> These learnings in the group experience tend to carry over, temporarily or more permanently, into the relationship with spouse, children, students, subordinates, peers, and even superiors following the group experience.[9]

I shall not go into examples of encounter group interactions, since Rogers's mushy description should be adequate for those who are not already familiar, at least in a general way, with what encounter groups are. The 1960s and 1970s saw the formation of hundreds of thousands of such groups, actively involving millions of Americans. Rogers estimates that the number of encounter group participants in one year, 1970, was probably three-quarters of a million.

Little careful and systematic study has been done of the effectiveness

9. Carl R. Rogers, *Carl Rogers on Encounter Groups* (New York: Harper & Row, 1970), pp. 7-8.

and consequences of encounter groups. Rather critical evidence on their effects is presented in what is apparently the first major book on the subject, *Encounter Groups: First Facts,* by Morton Lieberman, Irwin Yalom, and Matthew Miles. A review by Wayne Joosse succinctly summarizes the authors' conclusions regarding the claims typically made for this type of group on the basis of their study:

> The subjects . . . were Stanford University students. This is hardly a sample representative of the general population. Since it was weighted with bright, verbal young people, it favored therapeutic outcomes. The subjects were assigned in an essentially random manner (age, sex, and previous group experience were balanced) to 17 groups representing the ten major theoretical approaches (Gestalt, transactional analysis, Rogerian, etc.). Leaders were selected from among the most highly recommended in northern California, for some reason a particular stronghold of the encounter culture. (This quality leadership again favored misleadingly positive outcomes, for one of the ominous characteristics of the encounter movement is that, in the absence of certification laws, many groups are being "led" by those whose only training and experience is having been in a group before.)[10]

Only about one-third of the participants experienced positive changes. Roughly eight percent of the total group sustained "significant psychological injury."[11]

"Theoretical orientation" seemed to matter little, though "leader style" had a greater effect. The more empathetic and supportive leaders ("enlightened paternalism") achieved the greatest number of positive changes, while the more aggressive and "charismatic" leaders were correlated with negative outcomes. Distressingly, the leaders themselves were very poor at identifying those who became "casualties," exhibiting instead almost blind faith in themselves and in their techniques.[12]

10. Wayne Joosse, "Do Encounter Groups Work?" *The Reformed Journal* 24, 2 (Feb. 1974): 8.

11. Joosse, "Do Encounter Groups Work?"

12. Joosse, "Do Encounter Groups Work?"

RECOVERY GROUPS

America's newest group enthusiasm is the recovery group movement. Most recovery groups are based on what are called "Twelve Step Programs," originally developed by Alcoholics Anonymous. Many of the steps have a strong religious and moral component; these groups have been the first forms of American psychotherapy to introduce the religious and the moral — *two major and very positive accomplishments.* Nevertheless, many recovery groups have been strongly influenced by the encounter group movement and by much of American self-psychology. This self-preoccupation dilutes and distorts many of the positive aspects of recovery groups.

First, many of these groups foster narcissism by focusing primarily on the person's problems, both psychological and other, to an extreme degree. In many respects, people's testimonies about how bad their life has been and what they have done are more like theatrical productions than confession. Second, many of these testimonies focus primarily on what other people have done to them: the emphasis is on the self as victim. It is not uncommon for the mentality of a "pity party" to pervade the gathering. We have all seen talk show guests who regale the audience with their sad stories of abuse, and codependency, and so on and on. At the end, the audience often applauds, and one has the impression that these well-scripted confessions are performances that have made the person a celebrity victim.

A further criticism of the "Twelve Steps" is that the program involves a peculiar notion of God. Today's recovery groups operate on the notion that God is to be understood as each individual defines Him/Her/It. This kind of flabby "openness" is not only fundamentally heretical, from a Christian or Jewish perspective; it can also promote psychological harm. For certain people, God becomes little more than a narcissistic projection of their own needs and desires — and of their strange views. Some years ago, the popular ventriloquist Edgar Bergen had a "dummy" named Charley McCarthy. In these groups, God becomes some people's Charley McCarthy: they make God approve whatever they want approved. The notion of a God of justice whose "thoughts are not our thoughts," the fear of whom is "the beginning of wisdom," is seriously at odds with this sort of do-it-yourself deity.

SELF-HELPERS

The first important popularization of self-theory for individuals came in 1964 with the publication of Eric Berne's *Games People Play*, which was to sell over three million copies. Berne represents personality as made up only of ego states (non-ego aspects of personality are entirely ignored). These states are: (1) those which resemble parental figures; (2) those which are autonomously directed toward objective appraisal of reality; and (3) those which represent archaic relics — ego states fixated in early childhood that are still active. These states are usually called the Parent, Adult, and Child, respectively, with undesirable behavior being caused by the Parent and Child states. Speaking to one's "inner child" first became popular in this kind of transactional analysis. The popularity of Berne's book presumably reflects his ability to describe the transactions between people, or "games," with clarity and wit. His particular formulation of self-theory is known as transactional analysis. The goal of his therapy is to help people become autonomous adults characterized by spontaneity, unbiased awareness of reality, and candid intimacy with others.

Following from and developing Berne's theory was *I'm OK — You're OK* by Thomas Harris. This book has sold over a million hardcover copies and has gone through more than a dozen paperback printings. In this form of transactional analysis, too, the three ego states — Parent, Adult, and Child — are the three psychic actors, and again the goal is to develop creative and growing human relationships free from fear. Later transactional analysts have focused specifically on business success and winning in the game of life — "You were born to win" is the motif.[13]

Two other popular books in the self-realization category are Nathaniel Branden's *Breaking Free* and *The Psychology of Self-Esteem*. Branden's goal is to develop the personal autonomy and self-esteem essential to an individual's well-being. Similarly, Jess Lair in *I Ain't Much, Baby — But I'm All I've Got* proclaims that his book will help you "free yourself through this proven program of self-acceptance, self-enrichment and love." *Person to Person* by Carl Rogers and Barry Stevens would fit into this category, as would books presenting Frederick Perls's *Gestalt Ther-*

---

13. Jut Meininger, *Success Through Transactional Analysis* (New York: Signet, 1973); this book has gone through numerous paperback printings. The quotation, which is representative of the text, is from the book's cover.

apy.[14] To provide any kind of complete catalog of the various popular self-theories is almost impossible, since the public appetite for this sort of book seems insatiable. Bookstores now commonly have psychological self-help sections, where one will find numerous other titles similar to those covered here.

An interesting variant of self-help is assertiveness training — therapy aimed at making the shy, timid, or withdrawn person more capable of assertion in interpersonal situations. In a typical session the client is put in a role-playing situation where he or she can make aggressive, independent responses to the therapist, who plays the role of someone attempting to take advantage of him or her. The result of these practice sessions is presumably an increase in the person's self-assertiveness. Not only does this training value assertiveness, but it also frequently involves devaluing love. A best-selling application to the business world of the same philosophy of blatant self-aggrandizement was published by Robert J. Ringer under the title *Winning Through Intimidation.* This handbook for personal success argues that winning in business and personal transactions depends on assuming an intimidating and assertive posture. Ringer claims to offer a realistic program for personal success. The injunction that we are to be concerned with our neighbor's good he dismisses as a ploy used by others against us.[15]

EST AND FORUM

Although it has clearly been a very popular form of self-theory, est — Erhard Seminar Training[16] — introduced some significant new characteristics. (In the 1980s, est was renamed "Forum.") In the first place, est-Forum was primarily a business, efficiently directed by its founder and head Werner Erhard for the purpose of making a profit. Indeed, the internal discipline of the organization was so strong that its style of operation has been labeled fascist. Beginning in 1971, it grew to a multimillion-dollar operation, involving a core of highly

14. See Frederick S. Perls, *Gestalt Therapy Verbatim* (Lafayette, CA: Real People Press, 1969).

15. Robert J. Ringer, *Winning Through Intimidation* (New York: Funk and Wagnalls, 1974). See *New York Times Book Review,* 29 Sept. 1975, p. 17.

16. See Pat R. Marks, *est: Werner Erhard* (Chicago: Playboy Press, 1974). The information that follows was taken from various chapters of the book.

trained seminar leaders plus a staff of thousands of volunteers. Seminars were four-day marathon sessions with as many as 250 participants, who paid $500 to $700 for the complete series. The seminars required a disciplined, well-trained leader and participants who were willing to follow the rules obediently throughout the sixty-hour experience. These marathon sessions had similarities with old-style, lengthy revival meetings, but their setting, in fancy large hotels, was quite different.

Seminar leaders were trained to resemble as closely as possible both the teaching and the personality of Werner Erhard. The main goal of the training was to get the participants to "transform their ability to experience living." The key word is *experience,* since the main thrust is not on new ways to believe or think but on new ways to experience. To this end various techniques were used, all of which were centered around the participants' self. The techniques come from a variety of sources — encounter groups, Maslow, Gestalt therapy, Zen, and Scientology. Although a few techniques borrowed from Eastern religion give such approaches a distinctively "spiritual" flavor — at least by comparison with earlier self-therapy — the overwhelming emphasis is still on the self.

Listen to some samples of its remarkable philosophy, quoted from the book *est: Playing the Game the New Way,* by Carl Frederick, an est graduate.

> *You* are the Supreme being. (p. 171)
>
> "Reality" is a reflection of your notions. Totally. Perfectly. (p. 177)
>
> So you got the notion to play a little game with yourself. That is, you said to yourself, something like, "Gee, this is rather boring. Wouldn't it be more FUN to COMMUNICATE." So you created a WORD game. That's all life is — one big word game. Don't lie to yourself about it anymore. They even wrote it down, not long after the beginning. They said: "AND THE WORD WAS GOD."
>
> Of course it was. (pp. 168-69)
>
> Also notice that there isn't any right/wrong — it simply doesn't make SENSE to be unethical. (p. 174)
>
> You had the notion that communicating would be more fun. And you created all the rules. So you are responsible for the game as it is. All of it. (p. 190)
>
> And it has no significance. You're IT. Choose. It has no significance. Choose. Life is one big, "SO WHAT?" "CHOOSE." (p. 191)

This particular book ends with a pure Rogerian position mixed with a popularized existentialist concern with choice.

> Letting go of the notions "they" told you about, and creating your own. That's what aliveness is all about.
>
> You see, in my view, the sole purpose of life is to acknowledge that you're the source, then choose to BE what you know you are. It'll all flow from there.[17] (pp. 211-12)

If you think Frederick has trivialized and distorted the original message in his popularization, a comparison of his views with those of Carl Rogers will be revealing. For example, Rogers says explicitly: "I am the one who chooses" and "I am the one who determines the value of an experience for me."[18] Even more interesting is a comparison of Frederick's message with the weighty existential philosophy of Jean-Paul Sartre:

> If I've discarded God the father, there has to be someone to invent values. . . . To say that we invent values means nothing else but this: life has no meaning *a priori*. Before you come alive, life is nothing; it's up to you to give it a meaning, and value is nothing else but the meaning that you choose.[19]

Hundreds of thousands of well-educated, upper-middle-class participants have paid to hear this amazingly literal self-deification combined with a belief in the ability of the omnipotent self to choose happiness and health and thus win at the game of life. All this is done in spite of the belief that the game of life has no intrinsic significance or meaning.

SELF-HELP SEX

Although we have not mentioned it in our discussion to this point, one of the major ways of being receptive to experience and expressing love is through sex. All of the authors discussed so far have advocated openness to sex and active discovery and exploration of sex. Such enormously

17. Carl Frederick, *est: Playing the Game the New Way* (1974; New York: Delta, 1976); italics in original.
18. Carl Rogers, *On Being a Real Person*, p. 122.
19. Jean-Paul Sartre, *Existentialism* (New York: Philosophical Library, 1947), p. 58; see also Sartre, *Words* (Greenwich, CT: Fawcett, 1964), pp. 156-57.

popular manuals as Alex Comfort's *Joy of Sex* and *More Joy of Sex* owed much of their success to people influenced by self-theory. John Money, advancing a position similar to Comfort's, advocated what he called the new "recreational" sex, in contrast to the old "procreational" sex, no longer seen as functional.[20]

The connection between the "Money and Comfort" recreational theory of sex and self-theory came in part from the importance given by the latter to avoiding culturally determined inhibitions and to being open, especially to interpersonal and sensual experience. Then, too, sex is easily interpreted as an expression of love. Taken together, these factors have made sex a primary emphasis of self-theory. The essential guiding principle can be stated as sex in the service of the ego.

In the best-seller *Open Marriage,* authors Nena and George O'Neill argued that sexual fidelity should be redefined so as to eliminate the elements of duty and obligation, which they saw as threats to love, growth, and trust.

> Fidelity . . . is redefined in open marriage, as commitment to your own growth, equal commitment to your partner's growth, and a sharing of the self-discovery accomplished through such growth. It is loyalty and faithfulness to growth, to integrity and to self and respect for the other, not to a sexual and psychological bondage to each other.
>
> In an open marriage, in which each partner is secure in his own identity and trusts in the other, new possibilities for additional relationships existed; open (as opposed to limited) love was thought of as expanding to include others. . . .
>
> These outside relationships could, of course, include sex. That was completely up to the partners involved. If partners in an open marriage did have outside sexual relationships, it was on the basis of their own internal relationships — that is, because they have experienced mature love, have real trust, and are able to expand themselves, to love and enjoy others and to bring that love and pleasure back into their marriage, without jealousy.[21]

20. John Money, "Recreational and Procreational Sex," *New York Times,* 13 Sept. 1975, p. 23.

21. Nena O'Neill and George O'Neill, *Open Marriage* (New York: Evans, 1972), pp. 253-54. When the "open marriage" dissolves, one resource available for the devotee of popularized self-theory is Mel Krantzler, *Creative Divorce: A New Opportunity for Personal Growth* (New York: Signet, 1973).

Unfortunately, a few years after publishing their book, the O'Neills got divorced. Apparently neither was "mature" enough to follow their own advice.

The degree to which the argument for open sex in marriage quite naturally went was illustrated by Caroline Gordon's *Beginner's Guide to Group Sex*. This book took the O'Neills' thesis and argued aggressively that exchanging marriage partners for sex, euphemistically called "swinging," was a true sign of a good, mature marriage. After all, a self-fulfilled, non-jealous man and woman should be experience-seeking, relaxed about something so natural as sex. Gordon described the techniques and manners of group sex in sections with titles like: "What to Wear at an Orgy," "Who Does What to Whom and How," "Stimulants and Implements," and "Pardon Me While I Get My Boots and Whip." In sum, group sex is seen simply as a question of pleasure. The conclusion revealed just how casual these decisions were considered to be:

> Just as one shoe size does not fit everyone, neither does one cohabitation contract — or marriage contract — fit everyone either. It is best to explore and to discover what feels most "comfortable" to you and your mate. After all, the choice between Swinging and not Swinging is not irrevocable, anymore than sampling frog's legs is. If you find you like frog's legs, continue to order them, if you don't, you never have to try them again. Like frog's legs, Swinging can be continued, dropped, or practiced in moderation or abundance once tried. Each couple has the freedom to decide what best fits their taste.[22]

Despite the sale of millions of copies of the many guidebooks to marital and sexual satisfaction, the number of divorces climbed to all-time highs in the late 1970s and early 1980s.[23] The increase in the rate of divorce owes much to the values advanced by self-theory, at least if the comments of former partners can be taken at face value. Especially explosive is the combination of the values of self-theory with a strident version of feminism. Not surprisingly, women are insisting that they have

22. Caroline Gordon, *Beginner's Guide to Group Sex: Who Does What to Whom and How* (New York: Simon and Schuster, 1974), p. 156.

23. Divorces have levelled off and slightly declined since 1980-81; however, many observers attribute this to the large decline in the marriage rate. Millions of unmarried couples now live together, often for many years, but their break-ups are not counted as divorces. One example is the Woody Allen-Mia Farrow "family" tragedy.

the right to lead the same self-preoccupied kind of life many men have been living for years.

Perhaps it should be apparent that a high degree of assertive autonomy is impossible in any serious long-term human relationship, much less one involving the duties of genuine love and parenthood. As Christopher Lasch has noted, the idea of love as involving self-sacrifice and submission to a higher loyalty will "strike the therapeutic sensibility as intolerably oppressive," since "the mission of the post-Freudian therapies" has generally become the "gratification of every impulse."[24]

Madonna's recent book *Sex* has sold very well and has helped to bring sado-masochistic sex into the American mainstream — for her book is essentially an expensive "coffee table" S-M manual.[25] Another representative of the therapeutic gratification of every impulse is depicted in *The New Joy of Gay Sex*.[26] Here we have cheerful discussions of sex with children and sex with animals. You can also pretend you are making love to your daddy. After all, values and meaning are up to each of us. And besides, inhibitions, as we all know, are hard on our self-actualization — they are simply so ridiculous!

24. Christopher Lasch, *The Culture of Narcissism* (New York: Norton, 1978), p. 13.

25. Madonna, *Sex* (New York: Warner, 1992).

26. Charles Silverstein and Felice Picano, *The New Joy of Gay Sex* (New York: Harper Collins, 1992).

3. Selfism as Bad Science

From the description and commentary of the preceding chapter it is no doubt becoming clear that self-theory is a widely popular, secular, and humanistic cult or "religion," not a branch of science. We shall offer further evidence of the religious character of self-theory later, but for our present purpose of showing that self-psychology commonly functions as a religion it is appropriate to use Fromm's own definition of religion: "any system of thought and action shared by a group which gives the individual a frame of orientation and an object of devotion."[1] To place this in context, let us cite a very important example of the religious claims of humanism from John Dewey, the founder of today's dominant philosophy of education. Dewey concludes his book *A Common Faith* with an exhortation to make humanism an active "common faith": in humanism "are all the elements of a religious faith that shall not be confined to sect, class, or race. Such a faith has always been implicitly the common faith of mankind. *It remains to make it explicit and militant.*"[2]

Fromm's definition and Dewey's exhortation set in bold relief the aggressive ideological character of the kind of secular humanism we have been talking about, with its devotion to the "self" and to humanity. We shall use the term *selfism* to refer to this religion and its rationale for self-expression, creativity, and the like. We shall avoid terms like *selfishness* and *egotism*, which do not accurately describe the modern phenomenon and have in any event lost much of their critical sting.

1. Erich Fromm, *Psychoanalysis and Religion* (New Haven: Yale University Press, 1950), p. 21.

2. John Dewey, *A Common Faith* (New Haven: Yale University Press, 1934), p. 87; italics added.

Before taking up specific criticisms in the next chapters, let us note a very general one. Selfist psychology emphasizes the human capacity for change to the point of almost totally ignoring the idea that life has limits and that knowledge of those limits is the basis of wisdom. For selfists there seem to be no acceptable duties, denials, inhibitions, or restraints. Instead, there are only rights and opportunities for change. An overwhelming number of the selfists assume that there are no unvarying moral or interpersonal relationships, no permanent aspects to individuals. All is written in sand by a self in flux.[3] The tendency to give a green light to any self-defined goal is undoubtedly one of the major appeals of selfism, particularly to people in a culture in which change has long been seen as intrinsically good.

PSYCHIATRY, BIOLOGY, AND EXPERIMENTAL PSYCHOLOGY

The scientific criticism of selfism comes from three major sources: (1) psychoanalysis and psychiatry; (2) studies on animal behavior, such as those by biologists or ethologists; and (3) the research of experimental psychologists. All three disciplines make the same point: that aggression, including destructive aggression, is a natural, intrinsic property of humans, present from birth.

Psychiatrists of many persuasions reject selfism as a throwback to the optimistic, superficial, and completely conscious interpretation of mind common in the eighteenth and nineteenth centuries. One of Freud's widely acknowledged achievements was to conceptualize the powerful unconscious, irrational elements in human nature. Many have rejected his scheme of binary opposition between the life instincts (e.g., sex) and the death instincts (e.g., aggression). But the clinical evidence, assembled over many years from a large and heterogeneous group of people, for such behaviors as sadism, aggressiveness, narcissistic manipulation of others, repetitive and terrifying dreams, etc., is considered overwhelming. Instead of convoluted optimistic explanations about how society causes such things, it is simpler and more economical from a theoretical point of view to accept the intrinsic dual nature of humankind.

3. For a powerful defense of the unchanging character of Christian doctrine, see C. S. Lewis, *God in the Dock* (Grand Rapids: Eerdmans, 1970), chap. 3.

For example, the prominent psychoanalyst Melanie Klein based her theoretical system on the assumption that every infant is born with large amounts of rage, hatred, and envy.[4] These primal emotions are only reduced by the experience of love from the mother. In many respects, Klein assumed that each of us is born "bad" and that "good" only arrives from the outside, for example, from the experience of mother-love.[5] One does not have to take such an extreme position, and many other psychoanalysts do not, but even those who assume that the environment plays a great part in creating hatred, rage, and envy also assume that we are born with a strong tendency to react with these negative emotions once we experience frustration or other forms of pain.

In recent decades many psychologists and psychoanalysts have focused on narcissistic and borderline personality disorders. These seriously disturbed patients are commonly filled with enormous amounts of rage, envy, etc. As the depths of the human psyche get explored, it is becoming clear that our natural "sweetness and light" are at least matched by our natural bitterness and darkness. It was certainly no real shock in 1983 to most experienced clinical psychologists when the popular psychiatrist M. Scott Peck acknowledged the existence of evil and published his analysis of it in *The People of the Lie*.[6]

The position of Jacques Lacan, a prominent French psychoanalyst — that the ego's power is a kind of illusion — has been summarized as follows:

> Lacan's break with American ego psychology . . . is thorough. Whereas the American theorists have retained the Freudian notion of the ego as an agent of synthesis, mastery, integration, and adaptation, Lacan's point of departure . . . has been to revive a far more worrisome conception of the ego. . . . The Americans write of ego mastery, Lacan's ruse has been to situate that mastery in a (Hegelian) dialect of master and slave. What for the Americans is an agent of strength, for Lacan is the victim of the illusion of strength; the would be guardian of objectivity is the ideologue

4. Melanie Klein, *Envy and Gratitude* (New York: Basic Books, 1957). See also Otto Kernberg, "The Psychopathology of Hatred," *Journal of the Psychoanalytic Association* 39 (1991): 209-38.

5. See, e.g., J. R. Greenberg and Stephen A. Mitchell, *Object Relations in Psychoanalytic Theory* (Cambridge, MA: Harvard University Press, 1983), p. 135.

6. M. Scott Peck, *The People of the Lie: The Hope for Healing Human Evil* (New York: Simon and Schuster, 1983).

par excellence, whose main function is to insulate the ego from the scandal of primary process thinking [our unconscious psychology].[7]

In short, from the perspective of "depth" psychologists and others who work with the seriously disturbed, selfism is a superficial theory instrumental in producing occasional short-term positive effects in people who are already healthy or in those with only trivial neurotic difficulties.

Ethologists — for example, Nobel laureates Konrad Lorenz and Niko Tinbergen — fully accept aggression as one of the basic characteristics of animals, especially the primates, and humans in particular.[8] They see aggression as usually quite functional in maintaining social organization and in keeping other groups of the same species at a reasonable distance. Warding off predators also has obvious benefits. To an ethologist, aggression, like all traits, can be either "good," that is, functional, or "bad," that is, dysfunctional, depending on the circumstance in which it is being displayed. As for the claim that humans are naturally without aggression, that is preposterous. Indeed, our very success and dominance as a species strongly suggests that we have too much of it. Both Lorenz and Tinbergen believe that humans' aggressive capacity is now out of balance with recent cultural changes, and they carry on a lively debate over the exact nature of our aggression and how to control it. Even biologist René Dubos, a prominent humanist who shares many values with the self-theorists, nevertheless assumes that any analysis of human potential must start with aggression as a basic property of our character. He writes, "in view of the fact that human beings evolved as hunters, it is not surprising that they have inherited a biological propensity to kill."[9]

Ludwig von Bertalanffy is another prominent biologist and humanist who accepts the potential for good and evil as intrinsic to human nature. He argues on purely biological grounds that basic moral codes, such as those forbidding murder, rape, stealing, and the like, are needed for

7. Jeffrey Mehlman, "The 'Floating Signifier': From Levi-Straus to Lacan," in *French Freud: Structural Studies in Psychoanalysis,* Yale French Studies, 48 (New Haven: Yale University Press, 1972).

8. Konrad Lorenz, *On Aggression* (New York: Harcourt, Brace & World, 1966); Niko Tinbergen, "On War and Peace in Animals and Man," *Science* 160 (1968): 1411-18.

9. René Dubos, "The Humanizing of Humans," *Saturday Review/World,* 12 Dec. 1974, p. 76.

survival. Even strong positive bonds of comradeship and love are biologically needed. He notes that behavior consistent with such ethical
standards is common to many social animals and primitive human groups.
For Bertalanffy, basic ethics thus consists simply of verbalized instincts.
He goes on to develop an interesting interpretation of the basis of human
violence by arguing that the essential human characteristic is the ability
to symbolize. And it is the "clash between ideologies or symbols," not
the need for biological survival, that is the origin of war. In other words,
war is the natural outcome of human aggressiveness expressed in the
most distinctive human form — our symbol systems. The Old Testament
story of the origin of evil he finds remarkably accurate. He paraphrases
it in this way: "Thus man has to pay for the uniqueness that distinguishes
him from other beings. The tree of knowledge is the tree of death."[10]

That the expression of so-called positive drives like sex can be
dysfunctional is rarely considered by the popularizers of selfism or by
the major theorists. But today, the whole country is familiar with some
of the consequences of the self-oriented sexual revolution. In addition
to many millions of cases of sexually transmitted diseases (some of them
now untreatable, such as AIDS and herpes), countless cases of infertility
caused by pelvic inflammatory disease and other STDs, we have recently
witnessed the psychological community acknowledge that many sexual
behaviors are often a kind of addiction. Sexual addictions can include
uncontrolled visits to prostitutes, masturbation (both men and women),
uncontrollable pornographic viewing, as well as uncontrollable homosexual cruising.[11]

Other pathologies that may or may not be addictive include sado-
masochism. There is a substantial literature devoted to the joys of S-M
— for example, in such books as *Joy of Sex, More Joy of Sex, Group Sex,*
and *The New Joy of Gay Sex.* Books have appeared defending the thesis
that sado-masochism is fine if you like it — and if you haven't tried it,
don't criticize it.[12] Advertisements for this kind of behavior are promi-
nently displayed in such publications as *The Village Voice.* That in satisfying our biological hungers we often devour ourselves and others

10. Ludwig van Bertalanffy, *Robots, Men and Minds* (New York: Braziller, 1967), part
1, esp. p. 32.
11. See, e.g., Patrick Carnes, *The Sexual Addiction* (Minneapolis: CompCare Publications, 1983).
12. Gerald Greene and Caroline Greene, *S-M: The Last Taboo* (New York: Grove
Press, 1973).

receives little or no emphasis from self-theorists, despite the well-documented psychological principle that the adaptation level for pleasure (or the level for optimum stimulation) constantly moves up with experience. This "relativity of pleasure" pushes people to more and more extreme situations just to keep the amount of pleasure constant. In practice this leads to diminishing pleasure, because of the increasingly negative side effects of the more extreme conditions.[13] The psychologist Donald Campbell has noted in marriage and other personal relationships the common contemporary phenomenon of rising expectations of pleasure combined with a rising adaptation level, which can result in frustration of the sort that destroys so many present-day marriages. He suggests that a doctrine emphasizing duty instead of promising pleasure might produce an overall higher amount of satisfaction.[14]

Maslow has cited various types of evidence in support of his assumption that human nature contains only potential for good. Cofer and Appley, in their well-known text *Motivation: Research and Theory*, argue that this limited scientific evidence — for example, the unconscious regulation (or homeostasis) of certain body functions, self-selection of diet in children and animals — is only distantly relevant and quite weak. They write further:

> Other evidence for his view of human nature, suggested by Maslow, is that children are natural, spontaneous, undefensive, curious and, in their way, creative to an extent greater than the typical adult or older child in our culture. This is a point with which it is difficult to disagree, although we can find few satisfactory data that would directly validate it in other than an impressionistic way. Again, of course, it is difficult to say why such characteristics are taken as supporting a universal view of human nature without also mentioning that children are often irritable, impulsive, short-sighted, aggressive, egocentric and bound by physiological needs.[15]

13. See P. Brickman and Donald T. Campbell, "Hedonic Relativism and Planning the Good Society," in *Adaptation-Level Theory: A Symposium*, ed. M. H. Appley (New York: Academic Press, 1971). See also W. N. Dember and R. W. Earl, "Analysis of Exploratory, Manipulatory, and Curiosity Behavior," *Psychological Review* 64 (1957): 91-96; and Campbell, "On the Conflicts Between Biological and Social Evolution and Between Psychology and Moral Tradition," *American Psychologist* (Dec. 1974), p. 1121.

14. Campbell, "On the Conflicts Between Biological and Social Evolution."

15. Charles N. Cofer and Mortimer H. Appley, *Motivation: Theory and Research* (New York: Wiley, 1964), p. 682.

As for Maslow's well-known concept of "self-actualization," the relatively few studies that have investigated this notion have been far from supportive. For example, Maslow makes much of his assumption that self-actualized people are high in creativity. A test of this by Mathes,[16] however, found no evidence for this basic Maslovian assumption. Maslow also predicted that the self-actualized would tend to be physically strong, especially fit people. A study made to verify this prediction could find no support for it.[17] Other major difficulties with Maslow bear on his hierarchy of needs. As one personality psychologist pointed out, "There are people who are willing to suffer hunger and thirst... even to die for values Maslow assumed are less potent than the physiological needs."[18] Maslow's theory cannot account for this, and even his definition of self-actualization is inadequate. There is one paper and pencil test that measures individual differences in self-actualization, but it has been criticized for various serious problems, including a clear anti-religious bias.[19]

A further basic criticism of Maslow is that he assumed that the most fundamental human needs are physiological needs and needs for physical safety. The problem is that the one thing that a newborn infant needs more than *anything* else is obviously a loving mother. Unless the newborn baby is picked up and cared for, it will quickly die. Studies have also shown that babies whose physical needs are all well satisfied nevertheless fail to thrive and often die if they do not receive touching and holding — interpersonal attention. In short, from the beginning, love is inextricably connected to our bodily health, and it is arbitrary and misleading to imply, as Maslow does, that first you satisfy your physiological needs, then you satisfy your safety needs, then you satisfy your needs for love and belonging, and then you satisfy your self-esteem needs. There is no such reliable order.

16. E. W. Mathes, "Self-Actualization, Metavalues, and Creativity," *Psychological Reports* 43 (1978): 215-22.

17. R. M. Ryckman, M. A. Robbins, B. Thornton, J. A. Gold, and R. H. Kuehnel, "Physical? Self-Efficacy and Actualization," *Journal of Research in Personality* 19 (1985): 288-98.

18. Richard M. Ryckman, *Theories of Personality,* 4th ed. (Pacific Grove, CA: Brooks/Cole, 1989), p. 362.

19. P. J. Watson, "Apologetics and Ethnocentrism: Psychology and Religion within an Ideological Surround," *International Journal for the Psychology of Religion* 3 (1993): 1-20; see also P. J. Watson, R. J. Morris, and R. W. Hood, Jr., "Antireligious Humanistic Values, Guilt, and Self-Esteem," *Journal for the Scientific Study of Religion* 26 (1987): 535-46.

One final problem with self-actualization is that Maslow, at the end of his life, very clearly stated that self-actualization is found only in adults. He specifically said that the concept has no sensible application to children, and that even college students are poor representatives of self-actualization.[20] Much of the enthusiasm for self-actualization, however, has come from the public schools (the educators ignored Maslow's retraction). And even many of the studies attempting to explore the meaning of self-actualization have used college students as subjects.

Maslow was personally much more of a realist than his theories ever showed. He was quite aware of evil, and at the end of his life, in 1970, he was attempting to correct some of his own contributions to the "stupidities" of his day.[21]

In short, the empirical support for self-actualization is tiny compared to the widespread enthusiasm with which it has been embraced.

Carl Rogers initiated some of the first very primitive empirical studies of psychotherapy by tape-recording therapy interviews and analyzing the recordings, usually in a qualitative manner. He was also instrumental in some early investigations of patients' self-concepts using a technique developed by Stephenson called the Q-sort.[22] But despite the promise of these initial attempts, subsequent research by Rogers and his followers has been minimal. In fact, his emphasis has shifted so much in the opposite direction that he now attacks psychology as having a one-sided and arbitrary focus on methodology and research design.[23] In response, prominent clinical psychologists such as Hans Strupp have charged that Rogers and his followers are a major source of fuzzy-minded irrationalism and a serious threat to the scientific integrity of clinical psychology.[24]

When pressed, self-theorists argue that their ideas are in fact based on extensive empirical data — namely, the statements, emotions, and behavior of their patients or clients. The clinical setting, they claim, is

20. Abraham Maslow, *Motivation and Personality,* 2nd ed. (New York: Harper & Row, 1970), p. xx.

21. For Maslow's awareness of evil see *The Journals of A. H. Maslow,* vols. 1 and 2, ed. R. Lowry (Monterey, CA: Brooks, Cole, 1979). For his own "stupidities," see vol. 2, p. 1291.

22. Calvin Hall and Gardner Lindzey, *Introduction to Theories of Personality* (New York: Wiley, 1985), pp. 229-30.

23. Carl R. Rogers, "Some New Challenges," *American Psychologist* 28 (1973): 379-87; also see Rogers, *A Way of Being* (Boston: Houghton Mifflin, 1980).

24. Hans H. Strupp, "Clinical Psychology, Irrationalism, and the Erosion of Excellence," *American Psychologist* 31 (1976): 561-71.

a rich source of evidence that cannot be denied just because it does not fit the traditional rigid requirements for standard scientific experiments. This claim is very significant for Christianity and other religions as well, for if it is allowed, it means that the same criteria for what constitutes evidence are equally applicable to the encounters between clergy and the spiritually starved who seek their guidance.

The "clinical evidence" of the impact of conversion or spiritual rebirth has often been used to argue the validity of such experiences. Verbal reports (whether autobiographical or by witnesses) and the great joy, wisdom, and effectiveness of the saints constitute some of the major traditional proofs of Christianity. We now hear that such observations, in this kind of setting and relationship, are considered to constitute acceptable scientific evidence.

It is not a satisfactory rebuttal to argue that this kind of evidence should merely be taken as the first stage of data collection, after which the more cautious, traditional, scientific procedure of hypothesis testing moves in to clean things up. Such a retort fails because (1) the claim offered in the case of self-theory is that this sort of evidence is acceptable by itself; (2) in the case of the self-theorists, twenty to thirty years have passed without any significant evidence of the more scientific stage developing; and (3) psychiatrists and clinical psychologists have argued recently that the traditional scientific position or paradigm is in principle no longer appropriate. For example, existential psychologists "question the theoretical role of all major movements in contemporary psychology: the assumption that the study of man can be wholly a natural science."[25]

The whole loss of scientific standards with respect to humanistic and related psychology is beginning to be appreciated even in the world of psychology textbooks. For example, one prominent text on theories of personality describes Maslow's theory as one in which it is "difficult to tell where the scientific leaves off and the inspiration begins."[26] Recent criticism of psychoanalysis — and, by direct implication, all theories of psychotherapy derived from evidence taken from the therapeutic session

25. Jacob Needleman, "Existential Psychoanalysis," in *The Encyclopedia of Philosophy*, vol. 3 (New York: Macmillan, 1967), p. 156. See also Jerome D. Frank and Julia B. Frank, *Persuasion and Healing*, 3d ed. (Baltimore: Johns Hopkins University Press, 1991); William Schofield, *Psychotherapy: The Purchase of Friendship* (Englewood Cliffs, NJ: Prentice-Hall, 1964); Thomas S. Szasz, *The Myth of Mental Illness* (New York: Harper and Brothers, 1961).

26. Hall and Lindzey, *Introduction to Theories of Personality*, p. 234.

— has shown that such psychology cannot be scientific even in principle. In other words, the basic situation for obtaining evidence — the therapeutic session — is so biased, so subjective, so uncontrolled that no information obtained from it can be evaluated scientifically.

To make matters even more interesting, many recent theorists of therapy have claimed that the process is a storytelling or narrative one rather than a scientific one.[27] These theorists (such as Donald Spence) see psychotherapy as the development of a kind of personal history, the truth of which can never be very well ascertained. In addition to Spence, large numbers of therapists accept the notion that psychotherapy is not scientific and never will be — a fact they even celebrate. That is, increasingly psychotherapists have abandoned or actively rejected the scientific and medical model even as an ideal.

The shift away from the scientific perspective is based on various kinds of arguments to the effect that neither the natural science nor the medical model of psychotherapy is adequate. Major theorists — for example, Frank and Frank — develop the case that psychotherapy is a persuasion process, in which suffering is relieved through the patient's faith in the therapist and by the therapist's warm, sympathetic support combined with experienced application of any of a wide variety of theoretical systems.[28] Although today's systems must have characteristics that will effectively justify the faith of the contemporary patient, the emphasis no longer falls on attempts to "prove the truth" of different theories of psychotherapy. Clinical psychologists used to argue strenuously that their discipline was a bona fide science in order to support its claim to truth (and to help it get millions of tax dollars in support and to justify insurance claims). Today many are describing psychology in categories indistinguishable from those used for religious cures and conversions.

There have been some thoughtful, systematic, and scientific attempts to conceptualize and evaluate whether psychotherapy works. The results are quite modest, especially in terms of the claims of the popularizers. Nevertheless, there is reasonable evidence that psychotherapy and coun-

27. Roy Schafer, *A New Language for Psychoanalysis* (New Haven: Yale University Press, 1976), esp. chap. 3; Donald P. Spence, *Narrative Truth and Historical Truth* (New York: Norton, 1982); Theodore R. Sarbin, ed., *Narrative Psychology* (New York: Praeger, 1986).

28. See, e.g., Frank and Frank, *Persuasion and Healing.* See also Sol L. Garfield and Allen E. Bergin, eds., *Handbook of Psychotherapy and Behavior Change: An Empirical Analysis,* 3d ed. (New York: Wiley, 1986).

seling do benefit a significant proportion of the people who have recourse to them. However, the benefits that occur are not due to the particular theories espoused by the therapists. Thus it doesn't seem to matter much if the therapist is a Freudian, a Jungian, a neo-Freudian, a humanistic, or an eclectic therapist in outlook. The evidence strongly suggests that benefits from psychotherapy come from common factors found in every type of therapy. Major factors that make a difference include the commitment of the client to therapy and the therapist's positive support of the client, combined with an ability (often based on experience) gently to challenge the client's distorted thinking and to facilite positive changes.[29]

The only exception to this picture is that there is some evidence that cognitive-behavioral methods, when applied to very specific psychological problems — for example, phobias, panic attacks, etc. — can be superior to the various forms of "talk" therapy.[30] (But these approaches are not part of humanistic self-psychology.)

ARE WE INTRINSICALLY ALL THAT GOOD?

Exactly how extreme are the convictions of the selfists about the total intrinsic goodness of human nature? The answer is: quite extreme. The popularizers whose books number sales in the millions almost unanimously assume the goodness of the self. They rarely even discuss the problem of that self-expression which leads to exploitation, narcissism, or sadism. The combination of passing over this unpleasant aspect and constantly articulating a clear message of "love and trust yourself and do your own thing" obviously accounts for a good deal of their popularity.

The theorists may hedge on this issue, but not much and not often. Hall and Lindzey, in their well-known text on theories of personality, describe Maslow's position as definitely implying that "man has an inborn nature which is essentially good and never evil."[31] Remember Fromm's earlier statement that humanist ethics would be untenable if the "dogma of man's innate natural evilness were true." And Rogers's optimism has consistently

29. Frank and Frank, *Persuasion and Healing*. See also Michael J. Lambert, David A. Shapiro, and Allen E. Bergin, "The Effectiveness of Psychotherapy," in Garfield and Bergin, eds., *Handbook of Psychotherapy and Behavior Change*, pp. 157-211.

30. Lambert, Shapiro, and Bergin, "The Effectiveness of Psychotherapy."

31. Hall and Lindzey, *Introduction to Theories of Personality*, p. 200.

brought with it the failure to treat systematically such problems as malignant aggression, sadism, and the narcissistic self. Two of Rogers's formal statements about his theory of therapy suggest the limits to which he goes. In his most important theoretical summary, Rogers postulates as fundamental processes central to therapy that the client increasingly feel *"unconditional positive self-regard"* and experience "himself as the *locus of evaluation*."[32] Nowhere in this work does he qualify these principles or identify those people or conditions to which they do not apply. Nor have I found such qualifications in any of his other writings. The encouragement to narcissism, solipsism, and self-indulgence is obvious.

Fromm was much more aware of the problem of evil and its theoretical importance to his position. He devoted a book, *The Anatomy of Human Destructiveness* (1973),[33] to argue his humanist position against rising criticism. In spite of its length, the work fails decisively at defending his particular form of "optimistic" humanism.

There are several major weaknesses in Fromm's argument. First, he divides aggression into two varieties: defensive, useful, "good" aggression; and offensive, malignant aggression. The latter is the only genuine evil, and it is due exclusively to exploitative society and is not part of human nature. The initial difficulty is that the very existence of exploitative societies is not seen as being related to human nature. If people are so good, how did societies get so bad? But there is another equally significant problem with this distinction: in real life few people, if any, can reliably make such a distinction in connection with their own affairs. We have a strong bias to misperceive the legitimate defensive reactions of others as hostile and offensive aggression. This tendency is common even in children as young as one year old, for whom the role of social factors is minimal. As such, this bias is at the heart of much destructive and malignant aggression. A significant part of what is meant by the theological concept of original sin is this bias that warps our judgment and our will.

Second, Fromm attempts to explain the character of certain well-known sadistic and malignant historical figures. His presentation fails to identify any important and unusual childhood environment that could account for the violence and evil they perpetrated as adults. If certain

32. Carl R. Rogers, "A Theory of Therapy, Personality, and Interpersonal Relationships, as Developed in the Client-Centered Framework," in *Psychology: A Study of a Science*, ed. S. Koch, vol. 3 (New York: McGraw Hill, 1959), p. 216; see also pp. 209, 213.

33. Erich Fromm, *The Anatomy of Human Destructiveness* (New York: Holt, Rinehart and Winston, 1973).

historical figures had terribly abusive fathers and/or mothers, this raises deeper questions: (1) Why should we hate those who abuse and hurt us? Why shouldn't we just avoid them like bad weather? (2) Where did abusive parents get their motives? That is, how did they get that way? To argue that they were all part of a generally exploitative society is far too vague. Besides, why should exploitative societies have such effects unless we are predisposed to develop a capacity for violence? In short, why should hatred and violence come so easily — so naturally?

A third major weakness is that Fromm's examples are all taken from extreme historical cases. This is no accident, since it carries with it the suggestion that evil is relatively rare. However congenial this is to Fromm's theory, evil is unfortunately a commonplace experience in the lives of ordinary people. Destructiveness, meanness, and hate are expressed daily in university academic departments, theological seminaries, government agencies, business organizations, assembly lines, and homes, in large cities and small towns. Vicious talk, the disguised knife in the back, and the like are acts of which even "nice" people are frequently guilty. The famed banality of evil comes from this ordinariness and pettiness. Violent thoughts and fantasies and pet hatreds are some of our most familiar and pleasure-giving activities. We treasure, even fondle them. History's great monsters are not necessarily worse than you or I. True, they have had access to great political power with which to further their intentions, and most of us have little access to such power, but the evil is much the same. Pandering to fantasies of violence and revenge is a favorite pastime all over the world; and when our own internal scenarios begin to bore us, we can turn to the immense supply of TV shows, films, and literature specializing in revenge and violence.

Fromm also fails to appreciate the factor of boredom in stimulating aggressive activity. One of the great appeals of violence and war is that for many it allows escape from tedium by providing an exciting outlet. Psychologist-anthropologist Ernest Becker describes historical motives for war in this way:

> Sometimes men went to war out of personal frustration in the tribe, to work off sexual jealousy and grief, or even simple boredom. Life on primitive levels could be monotonous, and warfare was often the main source of new experience, travel, real stimulation.[34]

34. Ernest Becker, *Escape from Evil* (New York: Free Press, 1975), p. 137. This book

Boys roaming about in small groups playing at war are obviously having fun, and they rarely evidence hatred or true violence in such games. Boredom or the need for stimulation as a motivating force has been seriously underrated as a factor in many of today's social problems — juvenile crime, drugs, sexual problems.

Finally, Fromm's biological evidence is extremely unrepresentative. He ignores evidence for fatal aggression within species; for example, male lions, like many male cats, are frequent killers of their young. This is also true for some male primates. Fromm never discusses the evidence that socially cohesive animals — chimps and baboons, for instance — often show both the most intra-group cooperation and the most extra-group aggression. But this selectivity pales beside his omission of evolutionary theories of society, including evolutionary theories of morality and ethics proposed by biologists.[35] In its extreme form, the argument of these scientists runs as follows: "The organism does not live for itself, its primary function is not even to reproduce other organisms; it reproduces genes and serves as their temporary carrier."[36] (Recall Bertalanffy's position that ethical principles are verbalized instincts.) One need not accept such radical biological reductionism to see nonetheless that our biological nature provides a theoretical basis for understanding society, one very different from the vague notions proposed by humanistic self-theory. The extreme form of the sociobiologists' argument is that biology determines much or all of our social structure and roles, just as it determines our eye color. For example, many sociobiologists emphasize strict determinism and the intrinsic and untranscendable selfishness of all individuals. Altruism is interpreted as biologically determined and as a disguised form of individual — or, more often, group — selfishness; that is, they make the opposite claim of the humanists, namely that humans are totally selfish.

In recent years, few psychologists have been arguing for the complete goodness of the natural self. Probably historical and social events have

---

and Becker's *Denial of Death* (New York: Free Press, 1973) provide a profound modern case for the tragic inevitability of evil — and thus a powerful rebuttal of denials of the existence of evil by Fromm and other selfist thinkers.

35. Edward O. Wilson, "Competition and Aggressive Behavior," in *Man and Beast: Comparative Social Behavior,* ed. J. F. Eisenberg and W. S. Dillon (Washington, DC: Smithsonian Institution Press, 1971).

36. Edward O. Wilson, *Sociobiology: The New Synthesis* (Cambridge, MA: Harvard University Press, 1975); quoted in *APA Monitor* 6 (Dec. 1975): 4.

been a major cause of this shift. For example, the Holocaust raised profound questions about the human capacity for evil. The world's terrible ethnic, racial, and religious conflicts in the Middle East, India, Eastern Europe, and Ireland, for example — and persistent, painful racial conflicts within the United States as well — have made the earlier psychologists' optimistic assumptions seem naive, even silly.

Let us conclude our presentation of scientific criticism of the position that human nature is exclusively or almost entirely good, and that evil is some kind of mistake by society, with some remarks made by social psychologist Donald Campbell, president of the American Psychological Association and advocate of evolutionary social and biological interpretations of human society. Campbell sees in contemporary American society a "non-optimal production of underinhibited, overly narcissistic and overly selfish individuals," for which psychology must take considerable blame:

> There is in psychology today a general background assumption that the human impulses provided by biological evolution are right and optimal, both individually and socially, and that repressive or inhibitory moral traditions are wrong. This assumption may now be regarded as scientifically wrong. Psychology, in propagating this background perspective in its teaching of perhaps 80 or 90 percent of college undergraduates, and increasing proportions of high school and elementary school pupils, helps to undermine the retention of what may be extremely valuable social-evolutionary inhibitory systems which we do not yet fully understand.

Specifically, he says, there is "social functionality and psychological validity to the concepts of sin and temptation and of original sin due to human carnal, animal nature."[37]

---

37. Campbell, "On the Conflicts Between Biological and Social Evolution," pp. 1120-21; see also the summary of Campbell's address in the *APA Monitor* 6 (Dec. 1974): 4-5. For responses to Campbell's address, see *The American Psychologist* 31 (May 1976): 341-84.

Many of the psychologists who responded to Campbell's address construed the central moral issue as that of the individual's well-being (expressed through actions rewarding the self) versus society's well-being (for which people give up their liberty to a moral code and become altruistic). But this is a very low-level conceptualization of the problem. The higher religions claim that, through love of God and through transcendent experience, the individual is dramatically better off. One important consequence of spiritual transformation is greater altruistic behavior. Thus, in the religious interpretation, the individual and society are not in conflict but are in fundamental cooperation.

4. From a Philosophical
Point of View

A QUESTION OF DEFINITIONS

From a philosophical perspective, the most obvious difficulty with selfism is that its proponents fail adequately to define or characterize their central concept — the self. The closest any of them come to recognition of this problem occurs in the writings of the existentialists; and even then there are severe difficulties, as we shall discuss below. In the case of the American self-theorists, this fundamental issue is essentially passed over. For them, the meaning of the concept of the "self" is self-evident. The "I" or "me," as each person experiences it, is accepted at face value as valid. Of course, many examples of selves engaged in actualizing themselves are given, but the examples do not resolve the basic difficulties.

For example, does the self spring out of biology? If so, why is our biological nature ignored by self-theorists? Instead, they provide such remarkable descriptions as this by Stevens:

> In the beginning I was one person, knowing nothing but my own experience. Then, I was told things and became two people. . . . In the beginning was I, and I was good. Then came an other I. Outside authority.[1]

Such a summary statement, with its total optimism about our basic goodness, with its assumption of a mysterious and undefined "I" ex-

---

1. Carl R. Rogers and Barry Stevens, *Person to Person: The Problem of Being Human; A New Trend in Psychology* (Walnut Creek, CA: Real People Press, 1967), p. 9.

pressed in the language of the biblical story of creation (Stevens's last two lines sound like a parody), and completed with the comforting rationalization that all bad is caused by others, is a masterpiece of woolly thinking. The obvious question of how other people, all born equally good, managed to develop the ever-present evil social forces and outside authorities is never discussed.

Another important problem of the self is this: Are there not many conflicting parts and layers of the self? Certainly conflict between different self-goals, different ideals, and so forth is a common experience. If so, which is the "real" self? How does one choose among the various selves? If it is claimed that there is only one "true" self, or that the different true selves do not conflict, what is the basis for the claim? How is the true potential of the self recognized? Does the concept of the self not contain a nature or essence that restricts authentic existence and therefore should be rejected? Is the concept of the self not in fact given by society — particularly modern Western society? The self-theorists apparently think not, since they are constantly contrasting the self with society, which is usually seen as the enemy.

Difficulties such as these have been raised for years. Although B. F. Skinner's own position is neither adequate nor consistent, one sympathizes with the objection he pointed out in a 1956 debate with Rogers:

> What evidence is there that a client ever becomes truly self-directing? What evidence is there that he ever makes a truly inner choice of ideal or goal? Even though the therapist does not do the choosing, even though he encourages "self-actualization" — he is not out of control as long as he holds himself ready to step in when occasion demands — when, for example, the client chooses the goal of becoming a more accomplished liar or murdering his boss. But supposing the therapist does withdraw completely or is no longer necessary — what about all the other forces acting upon the client? Is the self-chosen goal independent of his early ethical and religious training? of the folk wisdom of his group? of the opinions and attitudes of others who are important to him? Surely not.[2]

Rogers did not reply then — or ever.[3]

2. Richard I. Evans, *Carl Rogers: The Man and His Ideas* (New York: Dutton, 1975), p. lxxxv.

3. We should note in passing that the point of accepting evil as intrinsic to human

THE EMPTY SELF

The problem of the social nature of the self has received some serious attention in recent years. To make this point especially clear, I will summarize the analysis of Philip Cushman in his article "Why the Self Is Empty: Toward a Historically Situated Psychology," because I think that his particular portrayal of this issue is especially succinct and convincing.[4]

Cushman presents strong evidence that the "self" is basically a social construct and thus that the meaning of a self is defined by the group or historical context within which an individual lives. One consequence is that the self is therefore a kind of moving target, in that it constantly changes, evolves, etc., along with changes in social and historical conditions. Although certain aspects of the self may remain constant, much of it is a concept in perpetual flux.

He compares, often implicitly, the modern American construct of the self with earlier, more traditional concepts. For example, he proposes that the American self has slowly changed from an earlier version in which people had a need to save money and to restrict their sexual and aggressive impulses. By contrast, the new American self, emerging since World War II, has a deep need to spend money and to indulge impulses — known in the present context as "self-actualization."

The earlier self, according to Cushman, was much more focused on developing a moral and religious character, while the more recent self has been concerned with a secular personality. This recent self has also been more other-directed and less self-reliant and inner-directed. In addition, the earlier and more traditional self was rooted in interpersonal relationships, anchored in an extended family, in neighborhood and small

---

nature is not to justify hard-hearted or cynical tolerance of existing evil. Instead, it is to include this essential knowledge as part of the starting point for a higher wisdom. A brilliant start on this can be found in Becker's *Escape from Evil* (New York: Free Press, 1975), which is a development of the position articulated by William James in the following quotation, which Becker uses as an epigraph:

> There is no doubt that healthy-mindedness is inadequate as a philosophical doctrine, because the evil facts which it positively refuses to account for are a genuine portion of reality; and they may after all be the best key to life's significance, and possibly the only openers of our eyes to the deepest levels of truth.

4. Philip Cushman, "Why the Self Is Empty: Toward a Historically Situated Psychology," *American Psychologist* 45 (1990): 599-611.

town communities, and in religious faith. As modern economic and political changes took place, the family was reduced to the nuclear family, and, more recently, to the subnuclear family, with a single parent. In addition, many people today live isolated lives, far from family and friends, in urban environments; many people move about or get transferred in the corporate world with such frequency that lifelong interpersonal relationships have greatly shrunk.

Cushman's basic thesis is that the traditional self, stripped of its long-standing social identity, was essentially "emptied." The internal vacuum, created by modern society, was filled by two new social forces: psychology and advertising. Advertising — or what is called here the "consumer society" — functioned to satisfy the cravings of a self increasingly without identity. Thus, today we understand who we are by the products we use, by the images associated with those products, and by the expressive activities we buy, for example, our vacations and amusements — in other words, by what is more generally known as our "lifestyle." Cushman argues that psychotherapy, along with commercialism, has been called upon to give meaning and identity to people suffering from a sense of personal emptiness.

Like Cushman, I also claim that psychological theories have been explicitly developed and have been popular precisely because of this need. By providing theories of the self and of its actualization, they have filled the socially caused emptiness. For example, take the theory of Jung, who explicitly stated that the great majority of his patients were people in their thirties or forties for whom life had lost its meaning. Jung also acknowledged that most of these people were suffering a kind of religious crisis as well. The Jungian theory proposes that the personal and collective unconscious of the patient is filled with all kinds of personified forces. Everyone's unconscious includes archetypes, symbolized distinctively for each individual — archetypes of the Self, the Persona, the Shadow, the Anima or Animus, and a host of other figures such as the Earth Mother, the Wise Old Man, the Hero, and so on. In view of Cushman's analysis, I would like to propose that Jung can be interpreted as the theorist who fills up the person's empty self with a whole community of characters whose endlessly fascinating ways absorb patients for the rest of their lives. The internal psychological community has replaced external social relationships.

Cushman nevertheless believes that the contemporary self still remains, in many respects, empty — despite the ministrations of advertising and psychology. The reason is that psychotherapeutic relationships — one's dealings with one's therapist or one's recovery group — are not adequate substitutes for the older, traditional interpersonal identity. I would add that relationships with the Jungian characters derived from your unconscious also fail to satisfy the deep need for human community. And finally, it would be a rare person indeed who thought that the products we buy — and the images associated with them — could truly satisfy our need for personal identity. In short, the modern solution to the empty self is failing.

A BASIC CONTRADICTION

The existential concept of the self — as distinct from the more general humanistic psychological self — has been well described. For example, MacIntyre offers the following clear characterization of the existential self:

> The existentialist individual resembles the Cartesian ego without the *cogito*. Sartre inherited from phenomenology an explicit Cartesianism. In Sartre the individual as the knowing subject is the isolated Cartesian ego; the individual as a moral being is a Kantian man for whom rational first principles have been replaced by criterionless choices. Neither God nor Nature is at hand to render the universe rational and meaningful, and there is no background of socially established and recognized criteria in either knowledge or morals. The individual of existentialism is Descartes's true heir.[5]

MacIntyre's summary reveals that the notion of the existential self presents major philosophical difficulties. First, such a self — built on the concept of a criterionless choice — appears to be impossible. A choice based on no criterion is not a choice. At the least, this concept — so contradictory, so bizarre, yet so central to existentialism — should be developed before one accepts the existential self that depends on it. In practice, of course, criteria are accepted by everyone, often unconsciously; and the existential personal philosophy proceeds from them. But a consistent existentialism cannot allow the acceptance of any criteria — particularly unexamined criteria — because of the absurdity of exis-

5. Alasdair MacIntyre, "Existentialism," in *The Encyclopedia of Philosophy*, vol. 3 (New York: Macmillan, 1967), p. 153.

·tence. That is, no a priori or externally valid principles exist. Not even life itself is intrinsically meaningful.

Thus, a thoroughgoing existentialist could never begin existential life, for the process of choosing can never get started: the existentialist cannot get past the problem of the criteria for a first choice. Occasionally, existentialists have recognized this difficulty — as when Camus admits that the only important philosophical question is whether to commit suicide or not. Generally, however, the existentialist violates the principle of complete absurdity and escapes nihilism by assuming that the self, the process of becoming, and some other values (criteria) are valid and not totally meaningless.

This allows the system to get the process of choosing started, but it still leaves open the question of what the actual goal of self-actualization should be. What values and potentials among the many that are available to me should I or will I choose? When it comes to defining its famous "authentic self," existentialism is, by definition, no help. In practice, apparently, any social or political philosophy is an acceptable basis for actualization. The lives of the major existentialist writers bear this out dramatically. Martin Heidegger, perhaps the greatest twentieth-century existentialist, was a Nazi for a period. Karl Jaspers was a liberal. Jean-Paul Sartre was a Communist or Marxist of sorts for a while. Kierkegaard was a rigid conservative who approved the monarchical repression of the popular liberal movements of 1848. Nietzsche has been interpreted as everything from a fascist to a tormented humanist to an anti-Christ.[6]

The problem of the ethical relativism of existentialism and of much of the theory underlying American selfism has been obscured by the almost unanimous liberal humanism of the American self-theorists. But there is no reason intrinsic to self-theory that it should be associated with liberal humanist values. That it generally has been so far is due to its (usually unacknowledged) incorporation of assumptions and values from the Judeo-Christian heritage of the American theorists and the dominant liberal or socialist Western intellectual community of the last generation. As Americans have moved into a different and increasingly turbulent political and intellectual climate, the extreme heterogeneity of the personal, social, and political positions that are seen as consistent with selfism is now clear. For example, both white and black racism are perfectly consistent with self-theory.

6. MacIntyre, "Existentialism."

Let us look more closely at some of the major existential assumptions and the internal contradictions and difficulties they create. Existentialists accept the existence of the self *(Eigenwelt),* but like the American selfists they never develop a theory of how the self is conditioned by innate biological factors. They also appear to overlook the way in which the existential self is the product of a very particular modern Western society. Because of this twofold failure to work out how social and innate mental factors affect the self, the arena within which the existential self operates is substantially unspecified. Clearly such factors must condition the "authentic existential self." Without this knowledge, however, the quest for authenticity is so ambiguous as to be fatuous.

For example, because you did not choose them, all of the following — and many more — are not authentic: your age, sex, race, nationality, ethnic group, family, language; your unconscious personality traits (both the bad and the good ones); your passionate (or calm) temperament; your health, memory, height, weight, intelligence, quality of voice, nice (or bad) teeth, shape of nose, complexion, eye color, and so on. Relentlessly, layer after layer of the unauthentic you is stripped away until a self results that is like a totally peeled onion, of which all that remains is the pure spiritual power of life. In practice, most of today's selfists stop long before, at some inauthentic level; but those few who follow the logic out leave science behind and end in language often indistinguishable from the traditional idea of a disembodied soul.

Another major problem stems from the fact that existentialism has accepted "reason" — that is, logic, mathematics, and scientific inference — as an essential component of everyone's mental life. The a priori existence of reason provides evidence that at least one part of a person's existence — namely, his or her reason — already has an essence or nature; and this essence precedes the self's existence. Furthermore, the process of reasoning is central to our choices, by which (according to existentialism) our nature is developed. That is, reason has a nature that is present at the start of our existence, and it is through the operation of this a priori activity that decisions are taken and hence our nature (essence) as individuals develops. Therefore, to a significant degree, the essence of the self proceeds from the essence of rationality. The selfists' neglect of how reason precedes and determines the decisions involved in "choosing" the so-called authentic self can be seen as part of their tendency to ignore all biological or innate properties of humankind.

BROWNING'S CRITIQUE

Although Browning makes a number of telling criticisms of humanistic psychology, one part of his critique is particularly effective. He notes that Rogers and Maslow both transform self-actualization from a descriptive notion into a moral norm.[7] They slide from the description of what self-actualization is to the proposal that self-actualization is good — that it should be sought after — and finally to the assertion that self-actualization provides a recipe for solving all our higher moral problems. Rogers writes that whoever relies on the principle of self-actualization will discover "that it is a suitable instrument for discovering the most satisfying behavior in each immediate situation."[8] Later, Rogers said that those who rely on their tendency toward actualization will learn that "doing what 'feels right' proves to be a competent and trustworthy guide to behavior which is truly satisfying." In other words, self-actualization is a valid guide for making our moral decisions.

Maslow makes the same jump from the *description* of self-actualization to the *prescription* of it as a universal principle and guide for moral behavior. Maslow's answer to the question "What is good?" is "actualization"; "what is bad" is anything that frustrates or denies the essential self-actualizing nature of humankind.[9]

There are, as Browning makes clear, serious problems here. The first is assuming, without any independent rationale, that self-actualization is good; another is that self-actualization is a reliable moral guide for all or most moral decisions. Again, Rogers and Maslow provide no convincing evidence for these presumptions. A final and serious problem is that these theorists assume that different people's self-actualization can be achieved without conflict. They assume that there will be a marvelous harmony among self-actualizers. Browning summarizes this remarkably naive position:

> These ethical egoists [e.g., Rogers and Maslow] assume a kind of pre-established harmony in the world that functions in such a way . . . that the actualization of all potentialities is basically complementary, that differing potentialities can never really conflict.[10]

7. Don S. Browning, *Religious Thought and the Modern Psychologies* (Philadelphia: Fortress Press, 1987), chap. 4.
8. Quoted in Browning, *Religious Thought*, p. 69.
9. Browning, *Religious Thought*, p. 69.
10. Browning, *Religious Thought*, p. 75. Browning views the humanist psychologists

ETHICAL AND SCIENTIFIC
MISREPRESENTATIONS

A final, serious criticism along philosophical lines must address selfism's common tendency to represent itself as both a science and an ethic. The claim that self-theory is a science is invalid by any useful meaning of the term *science*, since humanist definitions no longer distinguish psychology and psychotherapy from religion, literature, political ideology, and ethics. Yet by keeping the name *psychology*, which has been represented as a science for decades, by having self-theory taught by psychologists (that is, experts) in countless university classes, and by vaguely suggesting ways in which self-theory might be tested, selfism has falsely benefited from the prestige and generally acknowledged special truth value accorded to any science.

A related weakness is the tendency of selfists to imply that psychology as a science has somehow verified the values of secular humanism found in self-theory. Many proponents of selfism are generally quite aware of the ethical character of their system. Indeed, they argue cogently that therapeutic psychology cannot possibly operate without values. This position is widely accepted by most thoughtful people today. But how do you demonstrate scientifically the intrinsic goodness of the self, the moral desirability of an "actualizing," "experiencing-in-the-present," "becoming-creative" self? Obviously, such values have not been scientifically verified. At present there is no satisfactory evidence that science can verify any value. Yet the aura of authority that psychology has derived from its scientific status is often used by those teaching selfism to imply that its concepts and values somehow have or approach a scientific truth status.

Here I speak from considerable personal experience. As a student I sat in many classes in which, a few weeks after listening to aggressive talk about psychology as "the science of behavior" or "the scientific study of mind," I heard lectures on "self-actualization" and "encounter group processes and goals." No questions were raised about whether the initial arguments for psychology's scientific status still held. As a young professor during the 1960s I taught courses on motivation and personality,

as ethical egoists, and thus is in essential agreement with Michael Wallach and Lise Wallach, *Psychology's Sanction for Selfishness: The Error of Egoism in Theory and Therapy* (San Francisco: Freeman, 1983).

in which lectures on the theories of Maslow, Fromm, and Rogers followed close after lectures on instinctual, hormonal, and biochemical interpretations of motivation. All of this was, and still is, typical of the curriculum in the so-called scientific study of motivation and personality. However, had I also lectured on Christian interpretations of human motivation as providing a reasonable, observationally grounded synthesis of the problems of the self, it would have been seen — and would be seen today — as an arbitrary and unacceptable intrusion of religion into a secular discipline that many still think of as a science.

I am currently teaching a graduate course on theories of personality, which covers many of the theorists dealt with here. Although the scientific understanding of these theories has waned over the last fifteen or so years, they are still understood as objective and as at least semi-scientific. One can criticize their philosophical, and perhaps even their moral, assumptions. But if one were to propose a Christian (or for that matter, Jewish) theory of personality, this would be seen as unacceptable. Oddly enough, however, one of the common textbooks on personality theory — one used at my own university — contains a chapter devoted to a Buddhist theory of personality![11]

---

11. Barbara Engler, *Personality Theories: An Introduction* (Boston: Houghton Mifflin, 1991), chap. 16: "Zen Buddhism," pp. 445-74.

5. Selfism and the Family

THE ISOLATED INDIVIDUAL

From the previous chapters it is clear that the concepts and values of selfism are not conducive to the formation and maintenance of permanent personal relationships or to values such as duty, patience, and self-sacrifice, which maintain commitment. There is every reason to believe that the spread of the selfist philosophy in society has contributed greatly to the destruction of families. It is certainly no accident that many case histories in selfist literature are people in conflict with their spouses or parents over some self-defined goal. With monotonous regularity, the selfist literature sides with those values that encourage divorce, breaking up, dissolution of marital or family ties. All of this is done in the name of growth, autonomy, and "continuing the flux."

I shall argue here that the social destructiveness of much of today's psychotherapy can be attributed to characteristics of the therapy process itself, although psychologists assume that social or personality characteristics are to blame when, for example, a client's marriage ends in divorce. The problem begins with psychotherapy's neurotic preoccupation with the individual patient. This is reflected in the absence during most therapy of representation for the children, spouse, parents, and the like. Therapists tend to identify strongly with their patients, much as in the traditional relationship of lawyers and clients. Yet there is no analogy in psychotherapy to the fact that in the legal relationship all the major interested parties have their day in court — at least some opportunity to state their side.

Overidentification with and excessive trust in patients has plagued psychotherapy from the very start. One of the most famous examples is

Freud's early belief that his patients' descriptions of having been sexually abused in childhood were in fact always true. To his surprise he learned, by way of outside information, that such reports were often false. The experienced therapist who knows the patient's background and is possibly even acquainted with some other members of the family can usually correct for such distortions, especially if a transference relationship develops (in other words, if the patient begins to relate to the therapist as though to a father or mother). Analyzing transference reveals how the patient is distorting interpersonal relationships, thus allowing the therapist to take these distortions into account. By contrast, in short-term, client-centered therapy, where the two parties are typically complete strangers, where the therapy is client-directed and rarely challenges the client's interpretation of the facts, where total trust is required by theoretical dogma, and where transference can hardly develop, little impediment exists to accepting uncritically the patient's account of things.

That these pressures in therapy tend to side with anti-family values would seem to be compounded further by the high proportion of psychotherapists who are themselves divorced or alienated from their family and traditional religions. Such therapists have a normal human desire for social confirmation of their own life-pattern and thus may be the more inclined to encourage such a pattern in others.

The danger of therapists talking their patients into having anti-family attitudes or even "memories" that are hostile to their families is not merely a theoretical one. Recently, there have been large numbers of people who have reported that they were sexually or physically abused as children — often by a parent or other relative. There is no doubt that many of these reports are true. Nevertheless, there is also increasing evidence that many such reports are not true.[1] We should always keep in mind that memories, especially early memories, are very unreliable.[2] It is common for young children to take as reality stories they have heard

---

1. *False Memory Syndrome Foundation Newsletter* — for example, the issue for January 8, 1993, vol. 2, no. 1; see also other issues of the newsletter. Address: 3508 Market St., Suite 128, Philadelphia, PA 19104.

2. Elizabeth F. Loftus, "The Reality of Repressed Memories," paper read at the Annual Meeting of the American Psychological Association, Washington, DC, 1992. See also Loftus, "Repressed Memories of Childhood Trauma: Are They Genuine?" *Harvard Mental Health Letter* 9, 9 (1993): 4-5; and Loftus, *Eyewitness Testimony* (Cambridge, MA: Harvard University Press, 1979).

from others or things they have seen on television or in movies.[3] Moreover, memories of childhood events that are retrieved years after the event often involve conflations of two or more people and settings. Indeed, many psychologists believe that all adult memories of childhood are hopelessly unreliable or determined primarily by the motivations of the person — or the person's therapist — at the time of recall. One of these motivations is often provided by pressure from a therapist who is theoretically committed to finding abuse behind every childhood memory. Quite recently, a number of patients have admitted to fabricating memories of childhood abuse under pressure from therapists, and no doubt many others will surface in the years ahead. There is even a society devoted to the defense of parents against false charges by their children (and others).

SELF-THEORY AND DIVORCE

Many self-theorists, especially Carl Rogers, give very little value to marriage — and indeed encourage divorce on theoretical grounds. Wallach and Wallach have effectively captured the Rogerian logic, and I will summarize the Wallachs' points here. Rogers states that "a relationship between a man and a woman is significant, and worth trying to preserve, only when it is an enhancing, growing experience for each person."[4] The Wallachs note the extreme individualism of this position and rightly ask: "What is to happen when one partner, say, becomes ill?"[5] One might also ask: What about the children? We now know that divorce takes a heavy toll on children, and good evidence suggests that as many

---

3. A Harvard psychiatrist has reported that, according to a survey of the Roper Organization, more than two percent of Americans "remember" being abused by space aliens. Even if the estimate of 5,000,000 Americans with such memories is rather an exaggeration, presumably many thousand do "remember" such abuse. One can only assume that these "memories" are derived from early TV viewing and other such events, since there is no reliable evidence for the existence of space aliens — much less for their alleged abuse of millions in this country alone. But the Harvard psychiatrist did urge people to take such reports seriously! (See the *False Memory Syndrome Foundation Newsletter*, 2 May 1992, p. 1.)

4. Carl Rogers, *Becoming Partners: Marriage and Its Alternatives* (New York: Dell, 1970), p. 10; quoted by Michael Wallach and Lise Wallach, *Psychology's Sanction for Selfishness: The Error of Egoism in Theory and Therapy* (San Francisco: Freeman, 1983), p. 160.

5. Wallach and Wallach, *Psychology's Sanction for Selfishness,* p. 160.

as a third of the children of divorce never recover psychologically.[6] Unfortunately, the price of many parents' actualization has been their children's destruction. The whole notion of marriage involving commitment is swept aside by the idea that, as soon as one person decides, correctly or incorrectly, that his or her actualization is suffering, it is time to leave. The divorce boom that began in America in the 1960s and crested in the early 1980s clearly owes much to this kind of thinking. For hundreds of thousands of American children, divorce can best be understood as a form of child abuse.

Perhaps we can summarize all this best by noting that a "Rogerian" understanding of marriage created the popular expression that marriage is a "nonbinding commitment." A nonbinding commitment is a contradiction in terms; it is as absurd as belief in a round square.

PARENTS AS THE SOURCE
OF OUR TROUBLES

The anti-family effects of selfism are compounded by the overwhelming theoretical bias against parents in various schools of psychotherapy. This bias has existed from the beginning with Freud's postulate of the Oedipus complex: that an intense hatred between father and son, first emerging in the child around the age of four, is the primary and universal experience in the formation of all male personality. What the father has done to merit this hatred is not especially clear. Apparently his crimes are to be married to the child's mother and to be big. Oedipal hostility can be neutralized through various means, for example, fear; but for many it is assumed to remain active throughout life, and it is always considered capable of reactivation. There is no corresponding emphasis on love of the father in Freudian or in selfist therapy — although the evidence of such love is certainly commonplace.

More recently, the theoretical preoccupation has shifted to the mother, who has been under a veritable conceptual barrage for being (take your choice) dominating, castrating, controlling, manipulative, seductive, emotionally dependent. The modern mother can't win either.

6. Judith S. Wallerstein and Joan Berlin Kelly, *Surviving the Breakup: How Children and Parents Cope with Divorce* (New York: Basic Books, 1980); Judith S. Wallerstein and Sandra Blakeslee, *Second Chances: Men, Women and Children a Decade After Divorce* (New York: Ticknor & Fields, 1989).

In the case of both parents, it is high time that these "explanations" be called by their real name — a new variety of the old prejudice known as "scapegoating." When will psychological theory be honest and large enough to allow us all the dignity of accepting that the fault is not in our parents — any more than it is in our stars — but in ourselves?[7]

The ghost of the Oedipus complex and of the bad mother can still be found in transactional analysis, where father and mother get collapsed into the unisex ego state called "Parent." In *I'm OK — You're OK,* for example, there is no doubt that the Parent, in spite of some good characteristics, is seen as the major cause of our troubles. The Child is described as vulnerable, but otherwise as innocent, happy, and good. Consider this passage, for example:

> Emerson said we "must know how to estimate a sour look." The child does not know how to do this. A sour look turned in his direction can only produce feelings that add to his reservoir of negative data about himself. *It's my fault. Again. Always is. Ever will be. World without end.*
>
> During this time of helplessness there are an infinite number of total and uncompromising demands on the child. On the one hand, he has the urges (genetic recordings) to empty his bowels ad lib., to explore, to know, to crush and to bang, to express feelings, and to experience all of the pleasant sensations associated with movement and discovery. On the other hand, there is the constant demand from the environment, essentially the parents, that he give up these basic satisfactions for the reward of parental approval. This approval, which can disappear as fast as it appears, is an unfathomable mystery to the child, who has not yet made any certain connection between cause and effect.
>
> The prominent by-product of the frustrating, civilizing process is negative feelings. . . .
>
> There is a bright side, too! In the Child is also a vast store of positive

---

7. O. H. Mowrer, in "Sin, the Lesser of Two Evils" (*American Psychologist* 15 [1960]: 301-4), quotes the following "Psychiatric Folksong" by Anna Russell:

At three I had a feeling of
Ambivalence toward my brothers
And as it follows naturally
I poisoned all my lovers.
But now I'm happy; I have learned
The lesson this has taught;
That everything I do that's wrong
Is someone else's fault.

data. In the Child reside creativity, curiosity, the desire to explore and know, the urges to touch and feel and experience, and the recordings of the glorious, pristine feelings of first discoveries. In the Child are recorded the countless, grand *a-ha* experiences, the firsts in the life of the small person, the first drinking from the garden hose, the first stroking of the soft kitten, the first sure hold on mother's nipple, the first time the lights go on in response to his flicking the switch.[8]

This myth of the intrinsically good and happy child (recall Maslow's similar assumption), with negative influences all coming from the outside, is a form of sentimentality almost touching in its naiveté. In fact, parents and society provide a whole array of positive influences: love, food, music, playmates, dances, nursery school, games, travel, crafts, stories. Such events not only give the child great joy; they are also the common, positive, observable, sustaining activities of a normal child's daily life. Of these experiences there is no mention. Nor are the negative experiences that the child provides for himself or herself—intrinsic to human nature from the start—taken into account. The one-year-old's first jealousy; the first hatred, expressed by striking at another child (activities that appear to be enjoyed as much by children as by adults); the ease with which children learn the concept "mine" and the difficulty they have in learning "yours"; children's extreme self-centeredness; their remarkable capacity to become totally demanding tyrants—all of this is ignored.

The efforts that parents and teachers put into helping children to share, to play together, to cooperate, and so forth are tributes to the natural negative capacity of children and to the natural positive influence of parent and society. Transactional analysis, by contrast, sees the child as a repository of predominantly not-OK feelings caused by the parents. The negative experiences are likened to tape recordings that are constantly replayed later in life. To escape entrapment in this horrible parent-caused past, Harris introduces a third ego state, also unisex, called the Adult. The Adult begins its development as follows:

The ten-month-old has found he is able to do something which grows from his own awareness and original thought. This self-actualization is the beginning of the Adult. . . . Adult data accumulates as a result of

8. Thomas A. Harris, *I'm OK — You're OK* (New York: Harper & Row, 1967), pp. 48-49; italics in original.

the child's ability to find out for himself what is different about life from the "taught concept" of life in his Parent and the "felt concept" of life in his Child.[9]

This self-actualization is described as a kind of marvelous computer process. The Adult is

> principally concerned with transforming stimuli into pieces of information, and processing and filing that information on the basis of previous experience.
>
> The Adult is a data-processing computer, which grinds out decisions after computing the information from three sources: the Parent, the Child, and the data which the Adult has gathered and is gathering.[10]

As one might expect, creativity has nothing to do with the Parent but originates in the Child's natural curiosity and is developed by the information-processing Adult. The Child provides the "want to," and the Adult provides the "how to," the essential requirement for creativity being "computer time," which is provided by the Adult. It is interesting that curiosity is considered a completely positive motive; its fundamental connection with aggression is passed over.

In summary, the basic plot of the transactional analysis morality play is that the poor, defenseless, but intrinsically happy, good, and creative Child, burdened by the mean old Parent, is saved from losing the "Game of Life" by a self-actualizing, information-processing computer called the Adult.

One of the major activities in recovery groups is for each member to criticize — attack — his or her parents and other family members. Recovery group members all discover that their family was, in fact, "dysfunctional." Indeed, the phrase "dysfunctional family" is one of the most frequently used in the recovery group world. This emphasis has become so extreme that recently it was stated that ninety-four percent of families are dysfunctional. Perhaps "dysfunctional" is understood so loosely that such a statement is meaningless — as if one were to say that ninety-four percent of all people are not completely healthy. On the other hand, without research, statistics, and other good evidence, such claims are so ridiculous that those who make them may be classified as modern snake-oil salesmen, selling the newest universal cure.

9. Harris, *I'm OK — You're OK*, p. 51.
10. Harris, *I'm OK — You're OK*, p. 52.

Let's look more carefully at the claims made by so many people that their family is the cause of their problems. First, let's reflect on the issue of whether the claims of, for example, abuse are true. There are many reasons to be suspicious of the testimony obtained in recovery groups and often in psychotherapy; some of these reasons were noted earlier. But a very crucial issue is that there is strong social pressure for each member of a recovery group to give testimony about how bad their family was. This confirms each member's understanding of his or her own problem, and it confirms the general theoretical or ideological biases of the whole movement. One should keep in mind that many of the charges about what parents did are quite extreme and are actually charges of criminal behavior. In spite of the gravity of these charges, the parents or other siblings are rarely there to comment on their validity, much less to defend themselves. In short, a recovery group environment is often that of a typical lynch mob.

But let us assume that the charges are true — and no doubt this is often the case. What is one to do with these facts, this knowledge? Is this really something worth dwelling on any more than is absolutely necessary? For example, it is clear that the general tenor of many recovery groups and of much psychotherapy is that the patient or client is a victim of traumas inflicted on them by others in the past. This victim status carries with it two serious and harmful consequences. First, victim status is fundamentally passive. It contains a lot of self-pity, and, above all, it reinforces a state of hypnosis in front of a cobra; clients remain fixated and fascinated by the demons in their past.

Second, this victim status brings with it a strong sense of moral superiority. Much of its appeal comes from the belief that the child is now more moral — better — than the parent. Many people in recovery groups judge their parents very harshly. They engage in frequent finger-pointing and blame-casting. They often make little or no attempt to understand what was going on in their parents' lives, to understand that their parents had parents, who had parents, all the way back to Adam and Eve, who made some mistakes themselves. Recovery group members frequently ask for mercy for their own failings and weaknesses — but they have little mercy or understanding for their own parents.

Furthermore, let's look at this in a Christian context. First of all, it is very clear that we are not to judge others: Jesus says this over and over, and in many different ways: "Don't worry about the speck in someone else's eye before you take the plank out of your own"; "Judgment is the Lord's"; "Judge not, that you be not judged." So to say "I thank God that I am better than my parents" is nothing if not pharisaical. Many of these people complain that their parents were too judgmental — for example, about the sexual behavior of others — but they are themselves even more judgmental about their parents.

CHRISTIANITY AND THE FAMILY

However simpleminded this theme of hostility to the parent, it has prevailed for so long that it has become second nature for today's therapists and for patients as well. Over and over we hear and read variations on a parody of the words of the returning Prodigal in Jesus' parable: "Father, you have sinned and are no more worthy to be called my father." The position that healing therapy can and should be built on love, gratitude, respect, and forgiveness toward parents is completely unrepresented in the selfist writings. Imagine a therapy that regularly strengthened a patient's family. Why not use therapy to rediscover what the members of a family have in common, to recall the forgotten truths the parents provided but the patient rejected, to remember the parents' attempts to help that were rebuffed by a peer-spoiled or self-spoiled child? Many young people today have committed more psychological atrocities against their loving but bewildered parents than vice versa. Indeed, among upper-middle-class families it is time to recognize the psychologically "battered parent" as a familiar syndrome.

In contrast to selfist psychology, traditional Christianity and Judaism actively support the family and the community. For the Christian, the family is the basic model for society. Father, mother, brother, and sister are common terms for Christians in both Catholic and Protestant communities. All Christians are brothers and sisters as members in the mystical body of Christ represented on earth by the mother church. Everywhere the social emphasis of the church is on integration and synthesis. Judaism's remarkably strong support for the family is also well known. Many have explained Jewish survival in terms of this reverence for family.

For Christianity, the family is a small-scale, living embodiment of much of its theology: God the Father, Christ the Son, Mary the Mother, and all of us as the children of God are prominent biblical themes. May we not then view an ideology that systematically denigrates or attacks the family, by structural analogy, as a force attacking Christianity? Consider, too, the central holy day of Christmas, which is a joyous celebration of motherhood and birth. May we not see that a psychologist advising abortion is acting in hostility against the deep structure of beliefs and meaning celebrated in the Christmas story? Recall that the young Mary was pregnant under circumstances that today routinely terminate in abortion. In the important theological context of Christmas, the killing of an unborn child is a symbolic killing of the Christ Child.

In the last decades the West in particular has become increasingly aware of how modern economic and technological systems cause pollution by treating part of the environment as separate from the rest. The analytic attitude (analysis means breaking into parts) that dominates contemporary science and technology soon destroys the pattern and integrity of the surrounding environment. My argument is that in an analogous fashion modern psychology has created widespread "social pollution" by its analytical (and also reductionist) emphasis on the isolated individual and its relentless hostility to social bonds as expressed in tradition, community structures, and the family.[11] It is no accident that it was modern industrial society which first reduced the extended family to the nuclear family, then reduced the nuclear family to the increasingly common subnuclear family of one parent, and now works toward the parentless family where the child is raised by government programs.

Of course, the conventional wisdom for some years has been that the family has failed—hence the growing number of people seeking psychotherapy. But what is failing is not the family; what is failing is modernism, with its analytic emphasis on the independent, mobile individual, caught up in narcissistic goals. This uncontrolled individualistic search for personal gratification is as destructive of social ecology as the uncontrolled quest for economic satisfaction has been for our biological ecology. The answer to the meaningless lives of today's young people is to reduce the number of children being reared in shattered or noncaring families. It is not likely that this can happen unless there is a change in widely accepted beliefs about the value and importance of the family and about social bonds in general.

11. Much the same point is made in Robert N. Bellah, Richard Madsen, William M. Sullivan, Ann Swidler, and Steven M. Tipton, *Habits of the Heart: Individualism and Commitment in American Life* (New York: Harper & Row, 1985), e.g., p. 284.

One hopeful sign is provided by those approaches to psychotherapy that are called "family therapy." This therapy of course assumes a theory of the desirable or ideal family, and it raises important religious and ethical questions. There are some dangers here, especially with some of the new definitions of family. Nevertheless, the concern with the family unit and with keeping it together is a concern with social integration and a welcome move away from the extremely self-centered therapies that have turned so many souls into narcissistic social atoms.

6. Self-Theory and the Schools

VALUES CLARIFICATION

This chapter presents a critical evaluation of what has been and still is the most influential model of moral education operating in the United States in recent years. That it is a self-based model should not be surprising. The specific approach, known as values clarification, was developed by Louis E. Raths and Sidney B. Simon in collaboration with several colleagues.[1] The model was first published in the 1960s, while its widespread use in the public school system came in the seventies and early eighties. But its influence is still prevalent today.

Very generally, values clarification is a set of related procedures

designed to engage students and teachers in the active formulation and examination of values. It does not teach a particular set of values. There is no sermonizing or moralizing. The goal is to involve students in practical experiences, making them aware of *their own* feelings, *their own* ideas, *their own* beliefs, so that the choices and decisions they make are conscious and deliberate, based on *their own* value systems.[2]

1. See L. E. Raths, M. Harmin, and S. B. Simon, *Values and Teaching,* 2d ed. (Columbus: C. E. Merrill, 1978); S. B. Simon, L. W. Howe, and H. Kirschenbaum, *Values Clarification,* rev. ed. (New York: Hart, 1978).
2. Simon, Howe, and Kirschenbaum, *Values Clarification,* back cover; also pp. 18-22. Italics in original.

This chapter was supported by a contract from the Department of Education, "Toward a Psychology of Character Education," and by NIE Grant NIE-G-84-0012 (Project No. 2-0099), "Equity in Values Education."

As this passage demonstrates, the values clarification approach is contrasted with the traditional explicit praise of virtue and condemnation of wrongdoing (referred to pejoratively as "sermonizing"). Simon and Raths reject as hopelessly outdated any form of "inculcation of the adults' values upon the young."[3] Direct teaching of values is outdated, they say, because today's complex society presents so many inconsistent sources of values. It is argued that "parents offer one set of should and should nots. The church often suggests another. The peer group offers a third view of values. Hollywood and the popular magazines, a fourth.... The spokesman for the new Left and the counterculture an eighth; and on and on."[4]

In the context of the confusing contemporary scene, the developers of values clarification reject teaching morality. They also reject indifference to the problem of values, since indifference just ignores the problem and leaves students vulnerable to unexamined influences from the popular culture. Instead, Raths and Simon and their colleagues argue that all students need to know is a process. By using this process, students will be able to select the best and reject the worst in terms of their own values and special circumstances.

To enable young people to "build their own values system," the Raths system focuses on what is conceived as the "valuing process."[5] Valuing, according to values clarification, is composed of three basic processes, each with subcategories, which are presented in the following order:

CHOOSING one's beliefs and behaviors
    1. choosing from alternatives
    2. choosing after consideration of consequences
    3. choosing freely

PRIZING one's beliefs and behaviors
    4. prizing and cherishing
    5. publicly affirming, when appropriate

ACTING on one's beliefs
    6. acting

3. Simon, Howe, and Kirschenbaum, *Values Clarification,* p. 15.
4. Simon, Howe, and Kirschenbaum, *Values Clarification,* p. 16.
5. Simon, Howe, and Kirschenbaum, *Values Clarification,* pp. 18-19.

7. acting with a pattern, consistency and repetition.[6]

Instead of teaching particular values, the goal is to help students apply the seven elements of valuing to beliefs and behavior patterns that are already formed and to those that are still emerging. The values clarification theorists propose classroom exercises designed to implement their process. The exercises, called "strategies," represent the major contribution of their recent writing.

SELF THEORY AGAIN

Raths and his colleagues specifically note the similarity of their basic orientation to that of psychologist Carl Rogers—one of our major theorists committed to self-fulfillment and to the innate goodness of the self.[7] Additional evidence that values clarification theorists don't accept any tendency to do evil or to harm others as a part of human nature is the very fact that they never even discuss the issue. Presumably, the problem of evil raises the issue of objective values, as well as the question of how to deal with the intrinsically flawed self—a self that is given absolute power in the values clarification model.

It is not just the previously discussed scientific evidence and theoretical reflection that discredit the "total intrinsic goodness" assumption. The growth of self-expression in our classrooms in the last two decades has not served to bring a glorious increase in student happiness and mental health. If anything, the great rise in student violence and the continued decline in student test scores are evidence that the opposite has occurred. In short, the assumption about the complete natural goodness of the self, which stands at the heart of the values clarification theory, is false. This weakness alone is

6. The order choosing, prizing, acting is from Raths, Harmin, and Simon, *Values and Teaching,* p. 30. For reasons that are not clear, in their very popular book *Values Clarification,* Simon, Howe, and Kirschenbaum propose a different order: first prizing, then choosing, then acting. This order is no accident or error, since it is stated with emphasis on p. 19 and brought up later in connection with one of the strategies (p. 36). In that book, little attention is paid to where students *got* their initial values; the primary emphasis is on prizing already-existing values. Thus there is no concern with whether or not the values of these young students are *worth* prizing. (That would obviously raise the disturbing prospect of objective criteria for values.)

7. Raths, Harmin, and Simon, *Values and Teaching,* p. 9.

enough to remove it as a sensible candidate for a theory of moral education.

The psychological and, one should add, educational assumptions of the values clarification theorists are rarely presented and to my knowledge never explicitly defended. But their premises are essential to the approach, and their basic assumptions about human nature and education can easily be inferred from the model. At the center of values clarification is the concept of the self, with a corresponding emphasis on self-expression and self-realization. The way in which this psychological notion of the self is related to the educational theory of the values clarification theorists has been nicely captured by philosopher Nicholas Wolterstorff. Here is his description:

> The fundamental theses are that each *self* comes with a variety of innate desires, interests, and motivations, that mental health and happiness will be achieved if these innate desires are allowed to find their satisfaction within the natural and social environment, and that an individual's mental health and happiness constitute his or her ultimate good. [Such theorists] characteristically stress the malleability of the natural and social environments. . . . What must be avoided at all costs, though, is imposing the wishes and expectations of others onto the self. Down that road lie unhappiness and disease. . . .
>
> The proper goal of the educator, then, is to provide the child with an environment which is *permissive*— in that there is no attempt to impose the wishes of others onto the child — and *nourishing*— in that it provides for the satisfaction of the child's desires and interests.

According to some, a permissive and nourishing school environment is all the child needs:

> Others, however, argue that persons characteristically develop internal blockages or inhibitions of their natural desires and interests, with the result that they fall into mental disease and unhappiness. . . . [T]he school should not only provide a permissive nourishing environment, but also work to remove inhibitions on self-expression.[8]

The advocates of values clarification hold this latter view. Their procedures aim to remove any inhibitions in the realm of values (all inhibitions

8. Nicholas Wolterstorff, *Educating for Responsible Action* (Grand Rapids: Eerdmans, 1980), pp. 17-18.

are negative) that students might have picked up from home, church, or elsewhere.

The view that the self is intrinsically good, that corruption comes only from one's parents and from society, arose at least in modern times with Rousseau, continued through the nineteenth century, and has culminated in the twentieth century, especially in the United States. In the recent past this self-expression or actualization theory of human nature has dominated much educational theory, even more than the field of psychology. From Rogerian therapy to Maslow's self-actualization to open classrooms to self-esteem programs and values clarification, "self theorists" as educators have sought to promote mental health and happiness through the magic door of "self-expression." If we develop unconditional trust among students (and between students and teachers), remove inhibitions, support moral relativism, and let each do his or her own thing, then all will be well. Unfortunately, such has not proven to be true.[9]

A PHILOSOPHICAL CRITIQUE

The actual moral position of values clarification is usually personal relativism: something is good or bad only for a given person. At other times the model seems to assume the still more drastic position that values don't actually exist — there are only things that one likes or dislikes. In both cases, it follows that blaming or praising anyone's values or behavior is to be avoided. The problem is that the relativist position involves values clarification in a number of very basic contradictions. Taken as a whole, these contradictions completely undermine the coherence of the system. The first basic contradiction is that, in spite of the personal relativity of all values, the theorists clearly believe that values clarification is good. That is, relativity aside, students *should* prize their model of how to clarify values. Raths and Simon attack the inculcation of traditional values by teachers. But they simultaneously urge teachers to inculcate values clarification. Indeed, when they argue for

9. For a powerful critique of Carl Rogers's ideas as applied to education, see the remarks by William A. Coulson, a former associate of Rogers, as quoted extensively in Pearl Evans, *Hidden Danger in the Classroom* (Petaluma, CA: Small Helm Press, 1990). Coulson's revelations and analysis are required reading for anyone trying to evaluate Rogers's effects on education.

their system they moralize and sermonize like anyone else. They criticize traditional teaching of values as "selling," "pushing," and "forcing one's own pet values" on children. But when it comes to the value of their own position, relativism has conveniently disappeared, and they push their moral position with their own sermons.

The second major contradiction in values clarification derives from the basic absurdity of moral relativism. This is beautifully identified by Wolterstorff, whose analysis follows.

When values clarification brings up the question of whether children in the classroom should be allowed to choose anything they wish, the answer is "No." Teachers have the right to set some "choices" as off-limits. But they have this right, not because the choices are wrong, but because certain choices would be *intolerable* to the teacher. As Wolterstorff cogently concludes, values clarification turns into arbitrary authority. This most disturbing "logic" is instructively portrayed by values clarification theorists themselves in the following example:

> Teacher: So some of you think it is best to be honest on tests, is that right? (Some heads nod affirmatively.) And some of you think dishonesty is all right? (A few hesitant and slight nods.) And I guess some of you are not certain. (Heads nod.) . . .
>
> Ginger: Does that mean that we can decide for ourselves whether we should be honest on tests here?
>
> Teacher: No, that means that you can decide on the value. I personally value honesty; and although you may choose to be dishonest, I shall insist that we be honest on our tests here. In other areas of your life, you may have more freedom to be dishonest, but one can't do *anything any time,* and in this class I shall expect honesty on tests.
>
> Ginger: But then how can we decide for ourselves? Aren't you telling us what to value?
>
> Sam: Sure, you're telling us what we should do and believe in.
>
> Teacher: Not exactly. I don't mean to tell you what you should value. That's up to you. But I do mean that in this class, not elsewhere necessarily, you have to be honest on tests or suffer certain consequences. I merely mean that I cannot give tests without the rule of honesty. All of you who choose dishonesty as a value may not practice it here, that's all I'm saying. Further questions anyone?[10]

10. Wolterstorff, *Educating for Responsible Action,* pp. 127-29; see also Raths, Harmin, and Simon, *Values and Teaching,* pp. 114-15.

From this startling example, we might suggest the following analogies: "You may steal in other stores, but I shall expect and insist on honesty in my store"; likewise, "You are not to be a racist — or a rapist — in my class, but elsewhere that is up to you." You may have "more freedom" somewhere else!

The only rationale for forbidding a particular choice in the classroom is that the teacher finds the choice personally offensive or inconvenient. And, of course, teachers (usually!) also have the power to enforce their will.

As previously mentioned, the values clarification theorists explicitly support the position that each student should choose and develop his or her own morality. That is, morality is relative to each individual. The advocates of values clarification should acknowledge — although they don't — that as a result their theory, their system, pushes and indoctrinates one particular interpretation of morality. Out of all the many different approaches to morality and to values, only theirs is singled out for approval.

A further major problem raised by a morality of personal relativism is that it explicitly rejects all absolute or nonrelativist interpretations of the moral life. In particular, values clarification represents a direct attack on traditional religious morality. For example, traditional Jews, Christians, Muslims, and Hindus would all reject values clarification. For that matter, the morality of Aristotle or any contemporary representative of such a "noble pagan" view is also rejected by those advocating values clarification. There is a serious political issue here. The public schools in recent years have given values clarification much support, and in so doing the schools have given the morality of personal relativism a privileged position. That is, the public schools have used tax money systematically to attack the values of those students and parents who believe that certain values are true, especially those who have a traditional religious position. Such a policy is a serious injustice to those taxpayers who expect that in the public school classroom their values will be treated with respect or at least will be left alone.

A CRITIQUE OF PROCEDURES
AND STRATEGIES

A major part of values clarification is comprised by the classroom exercises that exemplify the system in action. These exercises are called "strategies," and they are easily used vehicles for discussing and clarifying values within the framework of the values clarification philosophy. There are more than seventy strategies, and they have been a major reason for the popularity of the approach. Even those educators who are aware of the relativistic philosophy of values clarification have often used the exercises under the assumption that they are neutral tools with which to approach the topic of moral education.[11]

First, the strategies involve questions that are asked of the students, questions that embody the social ideology of a small segment of American society. The questions are reliably secular, relativistic, very permissive, openly antireligious, and generally ultraliberal. This is, of course, a perfectly legitimate position in American society — but it has no right to be accorded special status in our public schools.

In addition, the procedures always focus on the isolated individual, separated from family and society, making choices based on the clarity and personal appeal of each alternative value. Such a procedure, as Bennett and Delattre point out, strongly encourages the student to understand morality as self-gratification.

The common procedures of values clarification have other negative consequences. The procedural goal of having the teacher try to increase the number of alternative moral positions propounded by students on a given issue reinforces the idea that values are relative to each person. Each of the potential different values, for example, about premarital chastity is likely to be embodied by at least one of the students' peers. This makes it psychologically very hard to maintain a firm belief in any absolute value without experiencing painful peer rejection. It is very difficult even for adults to reject a belief without also seeming to reject the person who holds the belief.

Another type of bias in a values clarification strategy for use with adults is quoted from an article by Bennett and Delattre:

11. For strategies, see Simon, Howe, and Kirschenbaum, *Values Clarification*. For critiques of values clarification, see the following articles by Richard A. Baer, Jr.: "Values Clarification as Indoctrination," *The Educational Forum* 41 (1977): 155-65; "A Critique of the Use of Values Clarification in Environmental Education," *The Journal of Environmental Education* 12 (1980): 13-16; and "Teaching Values in the Schools," *Principal* (January 1982), pp. 17-21, 36. See also William J. Bennett and Ernst J. Delattre, "Moral Education in the Schools," *Public Interest* 50 (1978): 81-98; and Paul C. Vitz, "Values Clarification in the Schools," *New Oxford Review* 48 (June 1981): 15-20.

In *Priorities,* Simon "asks you and your family at the dinner table, or your friends across the lunch table, to rank choices and to defend those choices in friendly discussion." One example of Simon's "delightful possibilities" for mealtime discussion is this:

Your husband or wife is a very attractive person. Your best friend is very attracted to him or her. How would you want them to behave?

a. Maintain a clandestine relationship so you wouldn't know about it.

b. Be honest and accept the reality of the relationship.

c. Proceed with a divorce.

In this exercise ... [a]ll possibilities for self-restraint, fidelity, regard for others, or respect for mutual relationships and commitments are ignored.[12]

This example, with its biased and limited options, speaks for itself about the values clarification system.

RESEARCH EVALUATING
VALUES CLARIFICATION

In contrast to the clear negative side effects of values clarification just mentioned — for example, pushing a particular social ideology, encouraging self-indulgence, ignoring or rejecting parental values — the *direct,* intended effects of values clarification are very limited. Despite the high level of interest in and writing about this approach, only a small proportion of these writings represents focused, relatively rigorous research. In other words, much of the writing has been either of the how-to-do-it variety or general pleadings for the approach. There has been only modest attention to whether it actually does what its proponents say it should.

The advocates of values clarification have contended that their aim is not to change students' states of mind but their actual behavior. But when their definitions of behavior are articulated, we discover that the desired "behaviors" come close to states of mind. The proponents want students to overcome apathy, overconformity, flightiness, etc., and to acquire "purposeful, proud, positive and enthusiastic behavior patterns."

12. Bennett and Delattre, "Moral Education in the Schools," pp. 81-98.

(Note that all of these moderately positive traits can be directed toward either moral or immoral ends; for example, Hitler and Stalin were certainly purposeful, proud, and enthusiastic.) The practical fact is that most of the limited research on values clarification has been directed toward paper and pencil tests that evaluate students' states of mind. In these studies, some students were exposed to values clarification approaches, while other students were not. Then both groups of students were tested to see whether the experimental or control groups shifted their patterns of values toward becoming more positive, proud, and so on.

Leming has examined the relatively few good-quality studies of the values clarification approach.[13] He determined that these studies applied, among themselves, seventy separate tests of statistical significance to the data assembled (many studies applied two or more such tests). Of the seventy tests, only fifteen (twenty-one percent) showed that the experimental group moved significantly in the appropriate direction. In the other fifty-five tests, either there was no significant movement or the movement was in the wrong direction. Another thorough review of the research reported approximately similar negative conclusions about values clarification having any predicted effects.[14]

Thus it appears that, even in paper and pencil tests, values clarification does not typically produce the effects its supporters claim for it. This does not mean that values clarification has no effects; it only means that it does not appear to generate the effects its designers hoped to produce. Whether it promotes negative side effects on students and whether the effects it does produce are good or bad were not issues addressed in the evaluative research.

We must also, of course, be concerned with the question of whether the approach, if it does work, is a good idea in terms of its own assumptions. The obvious assumptions underlying the approach are *(a)* that it is important that people in general, and young persons in particular, believe strongly in whatever they value and *(b)* that the values they choose without adult intervention will be desirable or good. Neither common sense nor research supports these assumptions. Clearly, on

13. J. S. Leming, "Curricular Effectiveness in Moral Values Education: A Review of the Research," *Journal of Moral Education* 10 (1981): 147-84.

14. Alan L. Lockwood, "The Effects of Values Clarification and Moral Development Curricula on School-Age Subjects: A Critical Review of Recent Research," *Review of Educational Research* 48 (1978): 325-64.

many occasions, tentativeness and open-mindedness are normal and healthy characteristics — they suggest a willingness to learn or to consider both sides. In addition, when someone has a correct opinion and must carry it out in the face of resistance, then pride and certitude may be desirable. But under other circumstances, such characteristics can be associated with arrogance and dogmatism. As to the assumption that young people will usually choose good values without special instruction, as we noted above, this is a naive view of human nature. In fact, our opinions about important social issues are always largely shaped by the socializing environment around us. Thus, adolescent declarations to the contrary, young peoples' values are significantly affected by adult influences. If responsible adults, such as teachers, do not try to promote good values, then irresponsible sources — gangs, TV, or other media — may succeed in promoting bad ones, even if the youths who apply such values believe they are reaching their own conclusions.

A VIOLATION OF PRIVACY CRITIQUE

The techniques and strategies of values clarification often very seriously violate the privacy of the student and the student's family. In fact, parents disturbed by the loss of personal privacy have been some of the most vocal and effective critics of values clarification and related procedures used in the schools.[15] The exact nature of this important criticism has been spelled out by Professor Alan L. Lockwood,[16] and his analysis will be summarized here.

To begin with, for all Americans personal privacy is considered to be something of great value, and a general right to such privacy is assumed. Reasons for this are worth mentioning. Privacy protects us from public embarrassment or ridicule. "For example, consider the probability of hazing were it known that the captain of the football team slept with a tattered, old teddy bear. Similarly we could predict adverse social reaction were it known that a person, currently living in a racist community, were coming to believe in racial integration."[17]

15. See, e.g., Martin Eger, "The Conflict in Moral Education," *The Public Interest*, Spring 1981, pp. 62-80.
16. Alan L. Lockwood, "Values Education and the Right to Privacy," *Journal of Moral Education* 6 (1977): 9-26.
17. Lockwood, "Values Education," p. 10.

Privacy also helps to maintain our psychological well-being. We need privacy to get rest from the pressures and demands of life. We need time to reflect privately about our life. It is hard to imagine how this reflection could function if we were under frequent pressure to reveal our feelings, thoughts, and plans — often when they are only tentative and partially formed. Even more crucial to psychological well-being is the very private inner core of beliefs, hopes, faith, and ultimate secrets that everyone has at the center of their personality. To be forced to expose these to the public view is for most people to threaten basic psychological integrity.

Lockwood also notes that "privacy is . . . essential for preserving liberties characteristic of a political democracy."[18] Secret ballots, the right to assembly, and many of our other liberties are only possible if social and government surveillance is limited and our privacy is maintained. The right to privacy is, Lockwood mentions, not an absolute right, since there are many kinds of information that the state, the schools, and other public institutions need in order to function properly. Nevertheless, the right to privacy is a very important one, and invasions of it should never be allowed except when fully justified.

In order to maintain our privacy, we need to be able to control information about ourselves. This means that, when information is requested, one must be informed about what information is being requested and what it will be used for. That is, there must be *informed consent*. Certain ways of getting information undermine a person's informed consent. First, informed consent requires a mature judgment — something no child is likely to have. Second, the information being requested must be clearly specified. However, many psychological tests, such as projective tests, elicit information that the person doesn't know is being asked for — for example, when subjects are asked to respond to the Rorschach inkblots or when subjects are asked to complete sentences. In these situations people may reveal information about themselves of which they are quite unaware. Of course, if the person is doing this within the context of psychotherapy there is no violation of privacy, since the person has sought out psychological help and the therapist is trained in the use of such information and is legally bound to secrecy. But when a teacher, playing amateur psychologist, requests such information in a classroom setting, a violation of privacy is very likely.

18. Lockwood, "Values Education," p. 11.

Another way in which informed consent is violated occurs when the person giving the information is under strong group pressure to be especially open with personal information. (Again, if the individual in question has chosen to go into group therapy and knows this pressure is going to develop, there is normally no violation of the right to privacy.)

As Lockwood makes clear, many of the questions that are used in values clarification violate students' right to privacy. In particular, questions about the interpersonal dynamics of family life, about personal, emotional life, and about general worldviews — all are almost certain to invade one's personal life. Lockwood notes the following questions from the values clarification handbook:

> *Family dynamics:* What does your mother do? Does she like it? Is she home a lot? What disturbs you most about your parents? Reveal who in your family brings you the greatest sadness, and why?
>
> *Personal behavior and emotions:* Recall the last ten times you have cried. What was each about? Is there something you once did that you are ashamed of? What do you dream at night? The subject I would be most reluctant to discuss here is . . .
>
> *General world view:* How many of you think that parents should teach their children to masturbate? If your parents were in constant conflict, which would you rather have them do: get divorced and your father leave home, stay together and hide their feelings for the sake of the children, get divorced and you stay with your father?[19]

Clearly, the above questions are likely to violate the privacy of the child or the parents or both. Keep in mind that there is strong group pressure in the classroom setting where the questions are asked, that the answers will often become public knowledge in the school and community, that the children are too young to give truly informed consent, that the teachers or facilitators are untrained in psychology, and that the students — still less, the parents — have never agreed to participate in such a process.

To undermine privacy even further, values clarification questions are often open-ended in a way that makes them a projective technique. Lockwood gives these examples of values clarification sentences that students are to complete:

19. Lockwood, "Values Education," p. 18.

Secretly I wish . . .

I'd like to tell my best friend . . .

My parents are usually . . .

I often find myself . . .[20]

Lockwood concludes from his analysis that "a substantial proportion of the content and methods of Values Clarification constitute a threat to the privacy rights of students and their families."[21] The strength and clarity of Lockwood's analysis should make it clear that this criticism alone is enough to reject the values clarification approach to morality in any school where informed student and parent consent has not been obtained.

WHY HAS VALUES CLARIFICATION BEEN SO POPULAR?

Given the obvious serious problems with values clarification, a natural question arises: Why has it been so popular? And it has been very popular indeed. Values clarification theorists were enthusiastically received speakers at scores of education conferences. Their books sold hundreds of thousands of copies. Workshops showing teachers how to use values clarification in the classroom were common at countless national and regional meetings of teachers and educators. Tens of thousands of teachers were trained to use it. As a result, values clarification spread quickly throughout the country in the 1970s, and many aspects of it are still prevalent in school courses in the 1990s, especially those courses dealing with values or value-laden topics — for example, drug, health, and sex education programs.

The major reasons for the popularity of values clarification seem to be the following:

1. For the students, the many strategies required no prior preparation; they were easily grasped and led to spirited classroom discussion.

2. The teacher was only a facilitator — not a true teacher — since

20. Lockwood, "Values Education," p. 19.
21. Lockwood, "Values Education," p. 19.

there was no actual knowledge to be passed on. As a result, little preparation was required of the teacher, and exams were usually unnecessary. After all, there were no right or wrong answers. The spirited and active discussions implied that the class had been a success.

3. The entire philosophy of letting each student pick his or her own values fitted in easily with our consumer society. People picked value systems rather like they picked a magazine to read, a movie to see, or a brand of soap to use.

4. The alternative seemed to be the direct teaching of particular values, and this seemed almost impossible to do. It seemed impossible because the reasons justifying many values were no longer familiar to teachers or students and seemed easily rebutted. Teaching specific values required prior training and knowledge justifying particular values, but most teachers had never received this training or the appropriate knowledge. Finally, the only way to teach such values seemed to involve heavy doses of lecturing or sermonizing. This kind of teaching is hard to do and is often rightly unpopular with students.

5. Many teachers had come to believe that, in a pluralistic society, teaching any value might be illegal. That is, a parent might complain or even sue if a teacher taught a value that the parent rejected. Along with this fear was the belief — at least at first — that values clarification was value-free or neutral, as its proponents claimed.

CONCLUSION: WHY VALUES CLARIFICATION MUST BE REJECTED

In spite of the immediate appeal of letting each student pick his or her own values (personal relativism), the values clarification approach must be firmly rejected. The major reasons for this are that individual relativism leads to social anarchy and that it flies in the face of simple common sense.

The issue of social anarchy may sound abstract and distant, but it is actually concrete and in each citizen's backyard. For example, racism is perfectly okay in the values clarification system. Remember that to hate people because of their race or religion or ethnic background is fine as long as the student chooses it. To reject school itself, to say "yes" to drugs, to cheat on exams, to steal from your schoolmates — all of these choices are okay if values are up to each person. These behaviors cannot be rejected by values clarification advocates.

Common sense tells us that certain values (or virtues) are regularly admired and accepted as obviously valid. Everywhere such traits as honesty, altruism, heroism, hard work, and loyalty are admired, and the liar, the thief, the coward, the lazy, the selfish, and the traitor are rejected. In short, there are cross-cultural values and character traits that go with them. Furthermore, the other criticisms mentioned put the final nails in the coffin of values clarification. Recall that values clarification takes as a fundamental assumption that the self is entirely good, without the slightest tendency to harm or exploit others. In addition, the strategies and exercises used in values clarification often contain particular ideological biases, and the questions used often violate the privacy of the student and the student's family.

Very simply put, the contradictions and incoherence of values clarification demonstrate that it is a simpleminded, intellectually incompetent system. In schools throughout the country, primarily because of parental protest, values clarification has lost some of its acceptance; nevertheless, its widespread success reveals the disturbing prevalence of a confused moral relativism in much of American education.[22]

Unfortunately, this moral relativism based on the complete autonomy of the self remains, even today, a part of many programs. The name "values clarification" is gone — but the same self-oriented moral relativism, under other names, continues to undermine the moral life of our children. Be on your guard against programs that focus on "deciding," "choosing," "decision making," etc. Programs that emphasize the *process* of deciding, and ignore the *content* of what is chosen, are almost always relativistic.

---

22. For a thoroughgoing analysis of the failure of moral education in today's schools, see W. Kirk Kilpatrick, *Why Johnny Can't Tell Right from Wrong* (New York: Simon and Schuster, 1992).

7. Selfism and Today's Society

A CREED FOR THE YOUTH
AND YUPPIE CULTURE

As we have already suggested, a serious difficulty with selfism is that, while it locates many psychologically important events in society, it never comes to grips with the question of who or what is responsible for society. This issue can be seen as particularly acute when these theorists' own ideas become integral parts of the same society they attack. Indeed, their favorite procedure for debunking earlier belief systems — calling them rationalizations and justifications of the social powers existing at the time they were formulated — can be turned with great effect on Fromm, Rogers, and Maslow. It is certainly no accident that self-growth emerged as a value in American society at a time when America was experiencing economic expansion on a scale unprecedented in human history — during the period from 1955 into the 1980s — bringing great wealth to more people than ever before. Nowhere was this heady growth more evident than in American colleges and universities, which filled up with more and more young people experiencing the usual growth in interpersonal life and intellectual development that characterizes people in their late teens and early twenties. What more natural belief system could there be than selfism — with its application of a Chamber of Commerce economic growth philosophy to mental life — in a society of burgeoning wealth that had long trumpeted the supreme value of the individual and the intrinsic value of change? The Yuppie decade of the 1980s, with an economy booming for so many, was understood even at the time as an expression of the "me" psychology first applied to the baby boomers in the 1970s. In short, self-psychology as a whole has supported, rationalized, and indeed greased the economic gears of our society.

Fromm has criticized what he sees as childish philosophical elements in the life and dogmas of medieval Christianity. But if the Middle Ages were childish, and if the Renaissance and Reformation (as Erikson says of Luther's revolt in particular) were similar to early adolescent rebellion,[1] one might then say that the last two centuries have been a late-adolescent identity crisis — a period when a kind of teenage or college-age philosophy is prevalent. People with such a worldview are characterized by a narrow rationalism on the basis of which they attack the beliefs of their childhood, by self-centered rebellion as a routine "romantic" attitude, and by extreme preoccupation with sex.

The pose of rebellion, the clichés of hostility to authority, and the enthusiasm for sex that have gone unchallenged for years in the modern world are wearing out. The time has come for a childlike philosophy to reassert its superiority to an adolescent one. A wise yet childlike way of life — that is how many of the highest religions and philosophies have been described. Such wisdom is, of course, far from identical with the actual worldview of children. Nevertheless, many important attitudes and beliefs of childhood are incorporated therein. There do not appear to be any forms of wisdom that enshrine the beliefs or behavior of youth, or the attitudes of those who are "thirty-something."

"A NATION OF VICTIMS"[2]

Because so much of self-psychology derives from and is dependent on the economy, people characterized by this kind of motivation are especially vulnerable when the economy goes sour. Their very identity is called into question when they no longer have either a job that allows some self-actualization or the money that is considered necessary for the same process. In the last ten or fifteen years, in spite of the generally growing economy, many Americans (in particular, those under forty) have found their economic and career hopes significantly frustrated. For some this has meant failure to advance to the level of their expectations;

1. Erik H. Erikson, *Young Man Luther* (New York: Norton, 1958).
2. Charles J. Sykes, *A Nation of Victims: The Decay of the American Character* (New York: St. Martin's Press, 1992).

for others it has meant a satisfactory but not very glamorous occupation — an occupation that looks increasingly like a "job," and less and less like a "career." For the first time in decades, it has meant for some a genuine downward mobility. The economy has grown — but certainly not as fast as people's expectations of success or even fast enough to absorb all of the large baby-boom generation. Whether the coming years will be better or worse remains to be seen. But we already have a large number of people for whom the economy, their career, and, one might add, their interpersonal relationships have been a serious disappointment. These people, in true self-theory fashion, see themselves as victims and look around for other people to blame.

The best description of our victim psychology is that provided by Charles Sykes in *A Nation of Victims: The Decay of the American Character.* Recovery groups are in many respects about learning that one is a victim, a victim of a dysfunctional family, or more specifically, of "toxic parents." Of course, we are all members of some minority, and that makes us in some sense victims of the rest of society, which is a kind of mythical majority. The growth of the notion that all of us have some kind of addiction, and the belief that addiction is a disease, places huge numbers of Americans in the victim category.

As we have lost our identity as members of traditional communities, such as family, church, neighborhood, or small town, we have found new identities of shared grievance. We are now "united" by being victims of everything from racism and sexism to "looks-ism" and "size-ism" to being adult children of alcoholics. America has become one huge circle in which everyone is pointing the finger of blame at someone else. Consider these absurd examples: a school district employee who was fired for always being late and who insisted that he was a victim of a "chronic lateness syndrome"; an FBI agent who embezzled $2000 from the government only to lose it to gambling, was fired, but then was reinstated — thanks to a court ruling that his gambling behavior was a "handicap" and thus was protected by federal law.[3]

We now have so many addictions that the total accounts for well over one hundred percent of the American population. The National Association of Sexual Addiction Problems (you probably didn't know there was such an organization) estimates that 25 million Americans are "addicted" to various types of sex. Sykes points out that apparently 20

3. Sykes, *A Nation of Victims,* p. 3.

million Americans are addicted to games of chance.[4] A leader of the codependency movement puts the number of adult children of alcoholic, abusive, or merely critical parents at more than 230 million. Eventually it becomes clear that the total of American victims is more than the entire national adult population. Sykes reminds us that millions of other Americans are victims of compulsive shopping syndrome, while others are addicted to such vices as eating chocolates and gossiping — and, I would add, complaining. In short, Sykes describes our country as having become a nation of whiners. There is much truth in the charge — and the phenomenon is heavily supported by self-psychology, which emphasizes only our rights and never our duties. After all, if one of our rights has been violated — and in view of the many rights we presume ourselves to have, this is inevitable — then each of us is a victim.

If the economy should take a really serious downturn for any period of time, the narcissistic pain of large numbers of Americans, who believe that life owes them an active consumer life of self-realization, would become overwhelming. And its political expression would become frightening, for we would have to find scapegoats to blame and punish. No doubt we would also find the political leaders who would know how to take advantage of our victim psychology.

SELFISM AND LANGUAGE

A distressing symptom of the spread of selfist ideas throughout our culture has been its effect on everyday linguistic expression. In conversation and in students' papers it has become common for "I feel" to be used in place of "I know" or "I think" — for example, "*I feel* that the conclusions were not justified."

A brochure on the life of Mother Elizabeth Seton, who was canonized as the first American-born saint, features in bold letters on its cover: "To her world she brought her self." It is not, of course, "her world," nor did she bring "her self" in anything like the completely autonomous way suggested by the copywriter. More religious, and far less selfist, would be the statement "To God's world she gave herself." The lyrics of the song "Oklahoma" — "We belong to the land, and the land we belong to is grand" — make the same point in a different way

---

4. Sykes, *A Nation of Victims,* p. 14.

and contrast with the popular but disturbingly possessive words of another song: "This land is your land, this land is my land, from California to the New York island. . . ." The idea of belonging to the land has been typical of people in all ages who are deeply attached to land and nature; the attitude disclosed by active personal possession "my land" is, by contrast, modern and selfist.

C. FitzSimons Allison makes this point about the active and passive voice with special clarity in two instances. In the first instance he reports that Albert Einstein once said in a conversation with Robert Oppenheimer:

> "When it has been once given to you to do something rather reasonable, forever afterwards your work and life are a little strange." This passive voice [Allison remarks], ". . . when it has once been given," has been used by extraordinarily creative persons since pagan times in exploring the source or genesis of their creativity. But the tide of modern times is going to the opposite direction.[5]

In the other instance Allison discusses a *National Geographic* report in which Alan Villiers retraced Darwin's famous voyage on the *Beagle.* Allison notes:

> In his narrative Villiers introduces a number of quotations from Darwin's diary. What strikes the reader is the difference in perspective between Darwin and Villiers. The former speaks of the ocean that "was here spread out," one species of bird "had been taken and modified for different ends," searching for the grand scheme "on which organized beings have been created," a special variety "had been modified for different ends." Villiers, a faithful representative of our age with its characteristic *hubris,* infers from Darwin's findings that all change, modification, and design is from within creation, autogenous, autonomous. He writes: "No wonder the local cormorant *has evolved* into a flightless bird. . . ."[6]

Selfism's active voice emphasis is contrasted by Allison with Christian worship, which "against all forms of idolatry is always and primarily rendered in the passive voice, in the expectancy and primacy of God's action and Word. In such worship we do not invent values but discern them. We

5. C. FitzSimons Allison, *Guilt, Anger and God* (New York: Seabury, 1972), p. 155.
6. Allison, *Guilt, Anger and God,* p. 156.

do not fashion our own identities but we are shaped and refashioned by the Spirit of God. Abraham, Moses, the prophets, and the disciples were all called. God's word came to them and their work was a response."[7]

PSYCHOLOGY FOR A CONSUMER SOCIETY

Rogers describes self-theory and encounter groups as radical, but their ready acceptance by millions of people makes this claim hollow. Selfism is in fact the perfect consumer philosophy, ideally suited for those with money and leisure. It is especially good for people who consume services such as travel, cuisine, and fashion. Early consumer advertising and the philosophy behind it aimed at selling things. Today's selfist emphasis, reflecting a later stage in consumer philosophy, is used to sell services and activities — that is, life-styles.

The material success of the contemporary economy underlies many of the assumptions that emerge in the selfists' writings. For example, Fromm may criticize the aggressive, competitive, and acquisitive character of the "marketing" personality produced by modern capitalism, but the selfist personality is in fact a creation of the material and social conditions of a late capitalist economy in which serious scarcity is, at least for most, a thing of the past.

Rogers, for instance, assumes that the general trend of human relationships found in contemporary America (especially the Los Angeles area), which is dependent on modern inventions and the associated urban economy, will continue to the same trajectory.[8] Typically, Rogers views recent changes in personal relationships as progressive. He cites with some enthusiasm his projections that by the year 2000 there will be truly effective computerized matching of couples, sex will have almost completely lost its role in procreation (that sex has major spiritual and religious significance is not even acknowledged), and effective long-term birth control techniques will be commonplace, so that lasting infertility of adolescents and marriages of various degrees of impermanence will be common.[9] He concludes his discussion of partnership with an exhortation:

7. Allison, *Guilt, Anger and God*, p. 156.
8. Carl R. Rogers, *Becoming Partners: Marriage and Its Alternatives* (New York: Delacorte, 1972).
9. Rogers, *Becoming Partners*, p. 8.

Any modern industry is judged in part by the size of its investment in R and D—research and development. It is recognized that a company cannot succeed unless it is eliminating past failures, exploring new possibilities, studying new materials for its products . . . [and is] supported by endless funds.

Experimentation is central to all technological advances, no matter how many traditions it overthrows. It is not only accepted, but financed and admired by the public. Change is the name of the game, and this is known and accepted by almost everyone.

Then he turns to the particular subject of the book:

Marriage and the nuclear family constitute a failing institution, a failing way of life. No one would argue that these have been highly successful. We need laboratories, experiments, attempts to avoid repeating past failures, exploration into new approaches.[10]

We shall bypass for now the religious and ethical issues raised by passages like this. Nor shall we scrutinize the assumptions made about the almost universal acceptance and admiration of modern technology. Instead, let us look briefly at some of the economic assumptions of Rogers's position. Clearly he accepts and admires the processes central to the modern economy, with its constant advance derived from research and supported by "endless funds" from an enthusiastic public. The arguments of no-growth economists, the ecologically grounded reservations about big cities and modern technology, the growing rational hostility to modern agriculture and big business—all are simply ignored.

An important example of the type of criticism that is utterly disregarded by the selfists is the intelligent and increasingly influential economic argument for a return to a simpler and less industrial society made by people like the Christian economist E. F. Schumacher.[11] Any such return to an environment resembling preindustrial society would suggest that social values and interpersonal relations might also become similar to those in preindustrial society. In any case, values and relationships in the future are unlikely to resemble a more extreme extension

10. Rogers, *Becoming Partners*, p. 212. Rogers's view of social experimentation as an aid to progress is an example of his debt to John Dewey, particularly Dewey's *The Public and Its Problems* (New York: Holt, 1927).

11. E. F. Schumacher, *Small Is Beautiful* (New York: Harper & Row, 1973).

of those found today. The selfists, by assuming business as usual, inadvertently acknowledge the dependence of much of their psychology on what many now see as a peculiar situation — the last stages of a late-industrial urban economy, which has already begun to decay.

It certainly proved convenient that, just as Western economies began to need consumers, there developed an ideology hostile to discipline, to obedience, and to the delaying of gratification. Selfism's clear advocacy of experience now, and its rejection of inhibition or repression, was a boon to the advertising industry, which was finding that the returns on appeals to social status and product quality were diminishing. Most of the short expressions and catchwords of self-theory make excellent advertising copy: *Do it now! Have a new experience! Honor thyself!*

Some of the clearest examples of selfist jargon in advertising are found in the pages of the popular magazines oriented to educated affluent consumers — magazines such as *Playboy, Penthouse,* and *Psychology Today.* Some representative copy for advertisements in *Psychology Today* ran:

> I LOVE ME. I am not conceited. I'm just a good friend to myself. And I like to do whatever makes me feel good. . . .
>
> . . . We live by a certain philosophy: We try to make our dreams come true today, instead of waiting for tomorrow. But before you can do good things for yourself, you have to know yourself. . . . You need self-knowledge before you can have self-satisfaction. Think about it.[12]

It is difficult to distinguish in these magazines between editorial philosophy and advertising copy.

Some years ago, as I was flying to another city, the self-based advertising struck me as especially frequent and odious. When I arrived at the check-in counter, I saw fliers and posters put out by the airline I was taking that assured me: "You are the boss, you are the boss!" Arriving at my destination, I picked up my bag next to an auto rental counter with posters that boldly stated: "Let us put you in the driver's seat!" As I left the airport, at a nearby intersection a fast-food restaurant was festooned with banners announcing "Have it your way!" It occurred to me at that moment that self-theory could be summarized as "the Burger King theory of personality": "Have it your way!"

But the past few years of inflation, recession, and economic tur-

12. *New York Times,* 28 Oct. 1975, p. 68.

bulence have driven home the point that selfism is heavily dependent on economic prosperity. It has become very hard to actualize ourselves at today's prices!

The call to self-indulgent appropriation of the benefits of prosperity is not always expressed as crudely as it is in these advertisements. Often it is cloaked by high-sounding motives. For instance, developing people's "creative potential" has been a standard goal for educators as well as psychologists for many years now. What is meant by "creativity" is that the adult or child express his or her potential, which is assumed to be intrinsically good (bad potential does not exist). They do not mean accomplishing anything of genuine creative significance. This worship of creativity seems to be an outgrowth of the Romanticism of the nineteenth century. What was worshiped then was the rare "god" categorizable as "the Genius." Gradually the "elitist" valuing of the Genius was transformed by American society into the inflated but comforting belief that the sacred creative self was centered in everyone. Our egos are all as worthy of worship as that of the Genius. Naturally, the supporting values of rebellion and defiant independence have been brought in as equally ideal for all of us. In the spread of this popular and flattering belief, creativity has been turned into a rationale for self-indulgence.[13]

---

13. For a Christian, however, all creativity comes from and belongs to God; to claim that a human being is *truly* "creative" is either silly or blasphemous. A person can express individual capacity in a creative fashion only by aligning himself or herself with God's will. Real human creativity thus requires a soul cooperating with God — a soul who becomes God's loving agent in all activities, however mundane. There is certainly no Christian basis for the massive egos so common in modern artists!

To the extent that there is a Christian concept of human creativity, the creative act is viewed as a gift: in creativity something is *given* — the greatest gift being life itself.

As secular humanism developed in the nineteenth century, the term *creative* began to be applied to great musicians, artists, poets, and thinkers — to those who gave others their music, paintings, works of literature, and scientific theories. But the divine component of creativity — present even in pagan culture in the concept of inspiration by the muses — has long since dropped out. Today, even the idea that creativity involves giving something to others is gone. Today, in the secular world, creativity is simply a gift from the self to the self; it has degenerated into a synonym for any form of personal pleasure, without reference to other people. I once heard a lecturer on sexual behavior seriously argue for the concept of "creative masturbation."

Hence, the claim that within the narcissistic logic of selfism being "creative" does not mean doing anything of genuine significance is accurate. In fact, a good case could be made for the net negative contribution to social, spiritual, and religious life by training

Robert Heilbroner has cogently argued the chilling case for economic and political disasters that could easily result in a new society in which sheer survival will be the primary goal. In considering the forecast of this new communal, much more agricultural, and perhaps even monastic society, Heilbroner writes:

> Talleyrand once remarked that only those who had lived in the *ancien régime* could know what *"les douceurs de la vie"* could be. He was referring to the *douceurs* [pleasures] of a court in which elegance and extravagance knew no bounds, and in which the wealthy and highly placed could indulge their whims and caprices with an abandon that we can only look back upon with the mixed feelings with which we regard the indulgence of all infantile desires.
>
> In our period of history, however, it may well be that the threatened *douceurs* are those of an intellectual milieu in which the most extravagant and heretical thoughts can be uttered. . . . Indeed, might not the people of such a threatened society look upon the "self-indulgence" of unfettered intellectual expression with much the same mixed feelings that we hold with respect to the ways of a vanished aristocracy — a way of life no doubt agreeable to the few who benefited from it, but of no concern, or even of actual disservice, to the vast majority?[14]

Our thesis is that self-actualization is a more generic term for what Heilbroner refers to as "self-indulgence" and the uttering of "extravagant and heretical thoughts." We need not assume the cataclysms and consequent future of Heilbroner and others who have made similar predictions to appreciate how great is the wealth needed for a society to provide for the physical conditions of self-actualization for even a small proportion of its people. Americans forget that we are, in terms of wealth, the upper-upper class of the world. The college campuses and Yuppie culture in the United States in the last three decades have shown all the frivolity and arrogance of the courts of the ancien régime. Like the French court, but on a larger scale, there has been in them little awareness

---

in creativity and self-actualization. Many people today have such high opinions of their "creative potential" that they prefer to live on welfare rather than to work at available but humble jobs — that is, jobs below their self-defined level of worth. Creativity programs have been schools in inordinate pride.

14. Robert L. Heilbroner, *An Inquiry into the Human Prospect* (New York: Norton, 1974), pp. 25-26.

of the fragile basis for the prosperity being enjoyed and of its dependence on people living far away. Instead, it is seriously proposed that self-actualization be a universal ethic for a future that is likely to raise the question of avoiding downward mobility — and possibly even of survival. "Let them eat cake" shines as a statement of compassionate realism in comparison with "Let them self-actualize."

8. Selfism and Christianity: Historical Antecedents

In the next three chapters we shall take up an explicitly Christian analysis and criticism of humanistic self-theories. We shall begin the process in this chapter with a documentation of some of the important historical relationships between the two faiths.

FEUERBACH

The popularizers of selfism, as far as I have been able to discover, never refer to the historical origins of their ideas. Thus they give the impression — so typical of American enthusiasms — that their ideas are genuinely new, the result of recent and extraordinary changes in technology and society.[1] What is in fact new in modern selfism is not its system of ideas, which is more than a century old, but the large number of people who now endorse it. Some of the particular applications and social consequences of selfism as discussed above are of recent origin as well.

The popularizers often acknowledge their theoretical debt to Rogers and to Maslow, less often to May and Fromm. But the writings of Rogers and Maslow show only the vaguest understanding of the work of the earlier theorists from whom their positions derive. May, no doubt be-

---

1. This is hardly the only case in which an idea originating in Europe has had its first large-scale application in America. Later, the large-scale effects often cross to Europe and are called Americanization. For example, a European invents the automobile, the United States creates the automobile society, which is then exported back to Europe.

cause of his experience and contacts in Europe, is historically more informed, while Fromm is by far the most scholarly and aware of his debt to nineteenth-century European thought, although even he neglects the central importance of Feuerbach to the humanist theory of the self.

Despite the historical character and secular trappings of contemporary self-theories, their origins are nonetheless closely connected to Christianity, frequently in a hostile way. Consequently, a brief review of these important historical connections will prepare the way for our explicitly Christian criticism in later chapters.

One important direct source for today's humanistic selfism is Ludwig Feuerbach's *The Essence of Christianity.* First published in 1841, revised in 1843, this work by a left-wing follower of Hegel became widely known for its influential attack on Christianity. Friedrich Engels described his response to the book: "One must himself have experienced the liberating effect of this book to get an idea of it. Enthusiasm was general; we all became at once Feuerbachians."[2] Among other later thinkers whose ideas about religion were directly or indirectly affected by Feuerbach were Marx, Nietzsche, Huxley, John Stuart Mill, Freud, and Dewey. The tradition of Marx, Nietzsche, and Freud leads to Fromm and May; that of Mill, Huxley, and Dewey connects directly to Rogers and Maslow.

The book consists of an argument against both the divinity of Christ and the existence of God, with the general premise that all theology be resolved into anthropology. Some representative quotations make clear the nature of Feuerbach's arguments and their similarity to those of today's self-theorists:

> Though theology does not realize it, man, by positing Christ as the God incarnate, has proclaimed that man's selfless love for humanity constitutes salvation. . . .
>
> . . . [T]he historical progress of religion consists in this: that which during an earlier stage of religion was regarded as something objective is now recognized as something subjective, so that which was formerly viewed and worshipped as God is now recognized as something human.
>
> But that which in religion ranks first — namely, God — is, as I have shown, in truth and reality something second; for God is merely the projected essence of Man.

2. Friedrich Engels, *Ludwig Feuerbach and the Outcome of Classical German Philosophy* (New York: International Publishers, 1941), p. 18; quoted in E. G. Waring and F. W. Strothman, eds., *Ludwig Feuerbach: The Essence of Christianity* (New York: Ungar, 1957), p. iii.

What, therefore, ranks second in religion — namely, Man — that must be proclaimed the first and recognized as the first.

If the nature of Man is man's Highest Being, if to be human is his highest existence, then man's love for Man must in practice become the first and highest law. Homo homini Deus est — man's God is MAN. This is the highest law of ethics. THIS IS THE TURNING POINT OF WORLD HISTORY.[3]

Engels and Marx considered Feuerbach's conception of humankind much too abstract and speculative, and they subsequently developed their familiar economic and political interpretation of human nature. Yet Marx acknowledges the debt he owes Feuerbach for his "dissolution of the religious world into its secular basis. . . . Feuerbach resolves the religious essence into the human."[4] It is interesting in this connection that Feuerbach first said, "Religion is as bad as opium"[5] — a view that Marx echoed in his famous attack on religion.

The case of Feuerbach indicates that in good measure today's humanist self-theories represent reformulations and extensions of the theses of earlier thinkers who were explicitly anti-Christian.

The relatively derivative character of contemporary self-theory will be clearer if we take a quick look at the hundred years between Feuerbach and the American theories.

AMERICAN SOURCES

In many ways selfism is as American as apple pie — perhaps even more so. (For example, see Kirk Kilpatrick's discussion of "The American Spirit.")[6] The psychological emphasis on the self is best understood as accentuating traditional American individualism, a theme that has always been part of American character — certainly since well before the Revolutionary War. But it is a theme that came into special prominence around 1840 in the writings of such figures as Walt Whitman and Ralph

3. Feuerbach, in Waring and Strothman, eds., *Ludwig Feuerbach*, pp. 26, 15, 11, 65.

4. Karl Marx, "Theses on Feuerbach," in Engels, *Ludwig Feuerbach*, p. 83; quoted in Waring and Strothman, eds., *Ludwig Feuerbach*, p. xii.

5. Engels, *Ludwig Feuerbach*, p. 47.

6. W. Kirk Kilpatrick, *Psychological Seduction: The Failure of Modern Psychology* (Nashville: Thomas Nelson, 1989), e.g., pp. 161-72.

Waldo Emerson. In many respects, Whitman is still considered the most distinctively American poet that we have produced. He is best known for a poem he called "Song of Myself," the first line of which — "I celebrate myself . . ." — could be a jingle for a kindergarten self-esteem program, although I guess "I'm the most important person in the whole wide world" makes the point a bit more clearly. Emerson, whose essay "Self-Reliance" was historically influential at the time, represents another aspect of this American individualism.[7] Apparently many American Christians think that the expression "God helps those who help themselves" is to be found in Scripture; it is not there, of course. Instead, this expression summarizes America's confidence in the isolated self, and the origin of this idea is purely secular. It has much to do with political rebellion, seeking independence from any form of external control, and it was pioneered by American political and social figures ranging from Jefferson and Franklin, to Emerson and Whitman, to John Dewey and Carl Rogers — none of whom, come to think of it, was ever especially known for his Christian faith.

Individualism in earlier American periods, however, was always mitigated and contextualized by two other traditions: one was the conservative "republican" concern for the common good and for civic virtue; the other was the Judeo-Christian tradition, with its emphasis on God's will, love of others, and the social expression of charity (our many hospitals are expressions of those concerns). Robert M. Bellah and his colleagues have very effectively described these three traditions and the dilemma of contemporary society, in which individualism has become massively predominant, while the other two traditions have withered.[8] It is the contemporary expression of this individualism which has reached extremes, and to which psychological theorists have contributed so much.

7. See Ralph Waldo Emerson, *Essays and Lectures* (New York: Library of America, 1983).

8. Robert N. Bellah, Richard Madsen, William M. Sullivan, Ann Swidler, and Steven M. Tipton, *Habits of the Heart: Individualism and Commitment in American Life* (New York: Harper & Row, 1985).

FOSDICK AND PEALE

Two prominent Protestant ministers, active during the period from 1920 to 1960, were — perhaps surprisingly — immediate precursors of individualist self-psychology: Harry Emerson Fosdick and Norman Vincent Peale. Neither is taken very seriously as a theorist, but they were important in popularizing psychological notions well before such figures as Maslow and Rogers.

Fosdick, a writer and preacher of wide influence, developed his ideas in New York City in the 1920s, 1930s, and 1940s — the formative place and period for most of American self-theory. A champion of liberal Protestant theology, he was also associated with Union Theological Seminary. We shall look at three of Fosdick's books that nicely summarize the development of his brand of self-theory. Not only are the basic ideas that he combined to create his theory interesting, but of even greater interest is the fact that these ideas were popular in a liberal Christian context before being widely published in the purely secular literature of psychology. That is, the first popular expression of such notions as "self-realization," "becoming a real person," and the like appears to have occurred in New York's Protestant pulpits.

The first book that is important for a summary of Fosdick's self-theory is *Christianity and Progress,* published in 1922. In a short preface Fosdick sets the tone for the book by describing the progress of the nineteenth century with the following words of Renan: "the substitution of the category of *becoming* for *being,* of the conception of relativity for that of the absolute, of movement for immobility."[9] The book itself develops this theme by assuming that the idea of progress — in both the material and social senses — had become not only the dominant but also the correct view of history. Fosdick argues that Christianity is intrinsically a progressive religion, and that therefore modern progress and Christianity are natural partners. By implication, Christianity is the religion of becoming, of relativity, of movement. The dangers of complacent optimism or of too simple a trust in progress are acknowledged, but the link of Christianity to dynamic progress is Fosdick's central message in this work.

Ten years later, in *As I See Religion,* Fosdick gives this answer to the

9. Harry Emerson Fosdick, *Christianity and Progress* (New York: Association Press, 1922), p. 8.

question, What is Christianity? "The divine origin, spiritual nature, infinite worth, and endless possibilities" of each "personality," he tells us, with its "power of intellect, creative hope and love," and "promise of development" constitute the "essential genius" of Christianity.[10] That is, the individual personality with all its promise for creative development is the central Christian concept. Given Fosdick's emphasis on the two ideas of progress and personality, one is hardly surprised that this line of thinking evolved by 1943 into a theoretical position much like today's selfism. Even the title of Fosdick's third and extremely popular book, *On Being a Real Person*, brings to mind the current situation, for Rogers entitled his most popular work *On Becoming a Person* (1961).

Before we summarize Fosdick's position briefly, we may note how his ideas developed. In the introduction Fosdick chronicles his deepening involvement over the years in religious counseling, mental health, and psychiatry. He addresses the book partly to ministers who face similar counseling problems but primarily to readers like those people who have come to him for help. *On Being a Real Person* is obviously an early variety of the psychological "self-help" book, and the author emphasizes his indebtedness to the many psychiatrists, neurologists, and psychological counselors who helped him over the years.

Fosdick begins, "The central business of every human being is to be a real person." This ideal of a "real person" he bases on a personality theory that is presented as follows:

> To be a person is to be engaged in a perpetual process of becoming. . . .
> The basic urge of the human organism is toward wholeness. The primary command of our being is, Get yourself together, and the fundamental sin is to be chaotic and unfocused. . . . When at last maturity is reached . . . , the whole organism can be drawn together into that "acme of integration" which appears in creative work.

Fosdick also makes the important observation that "in modern psychological parlance the word 'integration' has taken the place of the religious word 'salvation.'"[11] Integration, according to Fosdick, derives from self-discovery, self-acceptance, and self-love. It is expressed in creative activity and general well-being.

10. Harry Emerson Fosdick, *As I See Religion* (New York: Harper, 1932), chap. 2.
11. Harry Emerson Fosdick, *On Being a Real Person* (New York: Harper, 1943), chap. 2.

Fosdick's position contains Christian and religious vestiges, but in much of his theory of personality the ideas are thoroughly anti-Christian and difficult to distinguish from those of today's psychological self-theorists, especially Rogers. Indeed, one of the concepts Fosdick stresses is the discrepancy between a person's ideal self and his or her perceived or actual self. This discrepancy he views as the major cause of anxiety and fear. Self-acceptance and self-love will, he argues, remove this dysfunctional anxiety, and then, through integrated growing, a person can become his or her real self. Rogers is also known for his emphasis on the discrepancy between the actual and ideal self, but Fosdick in many ways preceded him on this issue.[12]

Where Fosdick got the concepts of self-realization, becoming, and integration is not clear. They were probably very much in the intellectual atmosphere in the period 1925 to 1945. Psychologists most frequently cited in *On Being a Real Person* are Alfred Adler, Gordon Allport, William James, and Carl Jung. Adler first introduced the notion of the "creative self," and thus he is probably an important direct influence. It may be relevant that Adler lost his ties with his Jewish background and in 1904 joined the Protestant church. Apparently he did this because he wanted to be part of a universal religion that was not restricted to a single ethnic group. There is no evidence of actual religious experience — much less a conversion — just an ethical and philosophical compatibility. Ellenberger reports that Adler "found it worthwhile to have discussions with a Protestant minister. . . . Adler acknowledged that both had much in common in the ideals they pursued, though one remained in the field of science [*sic*] and the other in that of faith."[13]

William James is often interpreted as setting the stage for today's self- and ego-theories, but the dynamic emphasis on becoming and integration is not especially Jamesian. Gordon Allport is known for self-realization concepts, but the publications in which he expounded them came years after Fosdick's book. Allport's *Personality: A Psychological In-*

12. See the discussion of Rogers in Calvin S. Hall and Gardner Lindzey, *Introduction to Theories of Personality* (New York: Wiley, 1985), chap. 6.

13. Henri F. Ellenberger, *The Discovery of the Unconscious* (New York: Basic Books, 1970), p. 595. Kurt Goldstein, whose organismic psychology emphasizes growth and integration, is another possible influence, as he lived in New York City from 1935 to about 1941. But Fosdick does not cite him, and since Goldstein's major relevant work, *The Organism*, was not translated into English until 1939, his influence on Fosdick was probably not significant.

terpretation (1937) is referred to by Fosdick several times, and this work is suggestive of such dynamic concepts.

Regardless of these influences, Fosdick was one of the earlier synthesizers of an interesting self-theory, and apparently he was the first by many years to make a self-theory the major thesis of a widely popular book — *On Being a Real Person* went through about thirty hardcover printings.

Norman Vincent Peale is primarily interested in case histories that demonstrate his dynamic "Positive Thinking" approach to life's problems. Still, he has to operate with a theory of personality, and, in spite of Christian components, this theory for Peale is essentially selfist in character. As early as 1937 Peale wrote: "The greatest day in any individual's life is when he begins for the first time to realize himself."[14] This assumption that self-realization is a central principle of personality is a constant in Peale's books throughout the next thirty years. He began *The Power of Positive Thinking* (1952) with these words: "Believe in yourself! Have faith in your abilities! . . . self-confidence leads to self-realization and successful achievement."[15]

Despite the frequent references to Scripture and Christian teaching (which give the book what wisdom it has), the overriding message and basis for its popularity is Peale's Christian rationalization of self-realization. The book's selfist character shines through its chapter titles: "How to Create Your Own Happiness"; "Expect the Best and Get It." This emphasis on having faith in the self reduces God to a useful servant of the individual in his or her quest for personal goals ("How to Draw Upon That Higher Power"). Many of Peale's case histories purport to demonstrate how prayer and faith have enabled someone to win in some competition or to gain business success.

Peale has generally been ignored as a thinker since his work is not especially scholarly. Yet the content and popularity of his message parallel that of Fosdick and many of today's secular self-help writers. Most of his books are now available in paperback, and they are widely featured in "self-help" sections of bookstores. Peale's formative period was also the 1930s and 1940s in the liberal Protestant atmosphere of New York

14. Norman Vincent Peale, *The Art of Living* (New York: Abingdon-Cokesbury, 1937), p. 10.

15. Norman Vincent Peale, *The Power of Positive Thinking* (New York: Prentice-Hall, 1952), p. 1; italics added.

City. Like Fosdick, he was strongly influenced by psychology, and his extensive experience in pastoral counseling led to occasional co-authoring with psychiatrist Smiley Blanton.[16]

To try to explain the appearance of an immensely popular humanist selfism in harmony with liberal Protestantism is a complex and interesting historical problem. As a rough approximation, what seems to have happened is that with the rise of secular ideas and values, especially psychological theories, the basic Christian concept of the unique importance of the self was stripped of its theological justification. Such traditional spiritual concepts as those which anchored the Christian self in experiences like prayer, contemplation, obedience, repentance, and mysticism — in faith — became so weak in mainline twentieth-century Protestantism as to be of little significance. The notion of pride as the fundamental sin — along with greed, envy, and the others — yielded to the belief that "the fundamental sin is to be chaotic and unfocused." The importance of the individual self was also enhanced by the political rationale of democracy and the popular secular tradition. However, a higher justification of the self required a more personal and less social and political rationale, and selfist humanism came in to provide the necessary "theory." Recall Fosdick's observation that integration and self-realization had replaced salvation.

The period of Fosdick and Peale was one of transition, in which a generation of faltering Christians, bored with and skeptical of basic Christian theology and ignorant of spiritual life, accepted an increasingly humanist notion of the self that had been dressed up with superficial Christian language and concepts. The emergence of the huge — and much more secularized — post–World War II generation signaled a new population that was ready for a pure selfism no longer associated with what was seen as the Christian preachiness of their parents' generation. In the United States the crucible for this transformation was the nation's educational system, as we shall discuss more fully later.

PIETISM

A final historical precedent is significant: the similarity documented by Thomas Oden of encounter groups to the Christian pietism and Jewish

---

16. For example, Smiley Blanton and Norman Vincent Peale, *Faith Is the Answer* (New York: Abingdon-Cokesbury, n.d.).

Hasidism of the eighteenth and nineteenth centuries.[17] Modern Protestant pietism originated in the seventeenth century and became a very significant religious and social phenomenon in the eighteenth and nineteenth centuries. In its various manifestations there was an emphasis on intense emotional response, usually occurring in small groups, but sometimes involving larger revival meetings. Pietism was a reaction against the arid, intellectualistic, authoritarian forms that Lutheran, Anglican, and Jewish established religions had taken. The period of its rise was, like our own day, a time of change and mobility, particularly on the American frontier. John Wesley's Methodist pietism is perhaps the best known, but there were many other forms, including Quakers, Shakers, the Harmony Community, and the Oneida Community. Communitarian societies were fairly common among the pietists, which suggests a similarity with today's "encounter" culture that Oden does not develop.

Oden thoroughly documents major similarities between pietism and encounter groups: the small-group format, a zealous pursuit of honesty, a focus on "here and now" experiencing, interpersonal intimacy, frequent long and intensive meetings (religious revivals and encounter group marathons). Oden presents the evidence for these factors through an extensive series of quotations from the literature of both groups. The following citations from pietist sources highlight similarities with encounter group psychology:

> They began to bear one another's burdens, and naturally to "care for each other." As they had daily a more intimate acquaintance with, so they had a more endearing affection for, each other. (Wesley, 1748)

> Let your expressions be clear and definite, pointed and brief, having reference to your present experience. (Newstead, 1843)

> Beware of resting in past experience. (Newstead, 1843)

> Self-examination, severe, thorough, impartial. The class meeting will be productive of but little real, lasting benefit without this. (Rosser, 1855)[18]

17. Thomas C. Oden, *The Intensive Group Experience: The New Pietism* (Philadelphia: Westminster, 1972).

18. Oden, *The Intensive Group Experience*, pp. 70-71.

Oden's conclusion that the encounter group culture is a demythologized, secularized Judeo-Christian theology is consistent with the case we have presented here. He goes on to develop a theological interpretation of encounter group ideology that is important and generally convincing. He argues that the underlying basic questions of encounter theology (for our purposes, read "selfist" theology) are:

I What are the limits of my being that frustrate my self-actualization?
II What possibilities are open for deliverance from my predicament?
III How can I actualize these possibilities in order to become more fulfilled?

This threefold sequence, which underlies effective psychotherapy and also recovery groups regardless of theoretical orientation, is expressed in Christian worship in the form of three acts:

I	II	III
Confession	Thanksgiving	Commitment

Some alternative Christian ways of representing this structure are: bondage → deliverance → mission; sin → grace → responsibility; the human predicament → the gospel → the life of faith.[19]

Oden's analysis provides another view of the religious character of selfism and raises the question of the particular historical relationship that existed between pietism and encounter ideas. Although the historical development of pietism and its connection to encounter groups and modern selfism need to be researched more thoroughly, Oden has provided enough information to question seriously Carl Rogers's claim that encounter groups are a social invention of this century.

THE SPECIAL CASE OF CARL ROGERS

Of the major self-theorists, Carl Rogers has probably had greatest impact. Robert Sollod, a clinical psychologist, contends that from an intellectual point of view Rogers is not so much a great innovator of ideas as "the

19. Oden, *The Intensive Group Experience*, pp. 103-5.

leader of a movement in which certain ideas are developed, promulgated, and explored under his aegis."[20] Rogers's ideas have undeniably been assimilated into the mainstream of American psychology, counseling, and education; and many young people have been drawn to encounter groups. Consequently, it is appropriate to single him out for special attention at this point, beginning with a short historical analysis of the origins of his ideas and concluding with a discussion of the significant religious character of Rogerian psychology.

Rogers, in the description of his professional and personal development, recounts a revealing event that occurred while he was still a student at Union Theological Seminary:

> A group of us felt that ideas were being fed to us whereas we wished primarily to explore our own questions and doubts and find out where they led. We petitioned the administration that we be allowed to set up a seminar for credit, a seminar with no instructor, where the curriculum would be composed of our own questions.[21]

He goes on to say that the only restriction was that, in the interests of the institution,

> a young instructor was to sit in on the seminar but would take no part in it unless we wished him to be active.... The majority of the members of that group in thinking their way through the questions they had raised thought themselves right out of religious work. I was one. I felt that questions as to the meaning of life, and the possibility of the constructive improvement of life for individuals would probably always interest me, but I could not work in a field where I would be required to believe in some specified religious doctrine. My beliefs had already changed tremendously and might continue to change. It seemed to me it would be a horrible thing to *have* to profess a set of beliefs, in order to remain in one's profession. I wanted to find a field in which I could be sure my freedom of thought would not be limited.

---

20. Robert N. Sollod, "The Origins of Client-Centered Therapy," *Professional Psychology* 9 (1978): 93-104; quote on p. 101. Much of this section is based on Sollod's paper. Sollod also documents the origin of the client-centered or nondirective technique in the work of Goodwin Watson, et al. — e.g., *American Journal of Orthopsychiatry* 20 (Oct. 1940) — and in the writings of Otto Rank and Jessie Taft.

21. Carl R. Rogers, *On Becoming a Person* (Boston: Houghton Mifflin, 1961), p. 8.

Sollod points out that the preceding paragraph prefigures — from a time before he became a psychologist — many of the major directions of Rogers's future thinking. Notice the emphasis on groups, the negative attitude toward authority and education as traditionally practiced, the desire that individuals find their own beliefs — which, it is assumed, will result in continually changing beliefs throughout life. There is also the assumption that change is good and that it leads away from tradition, authority, and religion. Rogers's personal move away from Christianity has remained as an implicit antireligious model in his subsequent writings.

In spite of his distaste for fixed doctrines, Rogers is a clear example of one who holds firmly to the fixed dogma that modern knowledge has rendered Christianity and other traditional religions permanently out of date. A corollary of this doctrine, rigidly held in much of the contemporary academic world, particularly by social scientists, is that the intelligent believer will sooner or later rebel from the faith. Indeed, on the basis of my personal experience, dating from the middle 1950s to the present, I would say that the abandonment of one's "religious background" was reliably assumed to be a rational consequence of getting an education, particularly in graduate schools. The basis for this assumption, of course, never came under the sort of systematic investigation, motivated by an honest quest for understanding spiritual or religious truth, that one might expect from the university, given the lofty ideals it professes. In brief, the antireligious prejudice expressed by Rogers in the passage quoted above was and still is a commonplace in the academic world.

If Rogers's early and rather intellectual "encounter group" experience was the kernel from which much of his later thought grew, where did he get the conceptual framework that was to provide adequate intellectual content for his position? Rogers suggests the link by stating that, after he crossed the street from Union Seminary to Columbia Teachers College, he came under the strong influence of the famous educator William H. Kilpatrick, an advocate of Dewey's philosophy, whom Rogers describes as "a great teacher."[22] The influence of Dewey on Rogers through the medium of Kilpatrick must have been very strong. Sollod notes the remarkable similarity of Rogerian theory as it later developed to the philosophy of progressive education to which Rogers

22. Rogers, *On Becoming a Person,* p. 9.

was exposed in his twenties.[23] The far-reaching parallels between progressive education and client-centered therapy extend to the very definition of human nature. It is as if the concept of human nature formed in Rogers as a result of his contact with the fathers of progressive education was the concept that he "progressively" developed in his own theories of therapy. Sollod makes the insightful observation that the close relationship between progressive education and Rogers's work can be demonstrated with excerpts from Kilpatrick's writings, in which one need only substitute the term "client" for "student" or "child," "therapy" for "education," and "therapist" for "teacher" to transform a quotation from Kilpatrick into a statement of Rogerian theory. The substitutions are italicized in the following Kilpatrick statements:

> I should like to think of *therapy* as the process of continually remaking experience in such a way as to give it continually a fuller and richer content and to give the *client* ever-increasing control over the process.

> You value *therapy* as it remakes life? Yes, as it remakes life here and now, I mean the *client's* life here and now. I am accordingly not so sure as to our old formal *therapies,* whether they best remake life. I fear they too often postpone remaking.

> We saw that growth and *therapy* were practically two ways of saying the same thing. This led to the redefining of *therapy* . . . as a process of continuous growth.[24]

Finally, Kilpatrick states a typically client-centered principle in these words: "Whether any piece of learning [read: *growth*] is intrinsic or not depends upon the pupil [*client*] and his need of such learning [*growth*], not upon the teacher [*therapist*]."[25] Kilpatrick does, however, give somewhat more emphasis to the teacher as a source of authority than Rogers gives the therapist. Still, the import of Kilpatrick's teachings is to encourage a trust in the free growth and learning of the student, in much the same way that Rogers was later to advocate a trust in the client.

Years later, Rogers made the circle complete by turning his interest

23. Sollod, "The Origins of Client-Centered Therapy," pp. 96-98.

24. William H. Kilpatrick, *Foundation of Method* (New York: Macmillan, 1926), pp. 191, 192, 198.

25. Sollod, "The Origins of Client-Centered Therapy," p. 98; quoted from William H. Kilpatrick, *How We Learn* (Calcutta: Association Press, 1929), p. 50.

to educational process and reform, basing this on his experience as a psychologist.[26] Unquestionably, Rogers's ideas are ones that Kilpatrick and Dewey would have smiled upon. Rogers himself acknowledges this link as follows:

> In one sense, our experience is a rediscovery of effective principles which have been stated by Dewey, Kilpatrick, and many others, and a rediscovery of effective practices which have certainly been discovered over and over again by competent teachers. Yet the fact that others have come to somewhat similar conclusions, not only in the recent years but in the more distant past, takes away nothing from the vividness of our own experience of discovery as we have tried to implement our therapeutic viewpoint in the field of education.[27]

In summary, the case of Rogers demonstrates the close and in many ways derivative connection between selfist psychology and the progressive philosophy advanced by Dewey, which still dominates much of America's educational system.

We have briefly noted in the preceding chapters that religious themes and language often surface in selfist theory. Let us look now at some of these prominent indicators of the religious aspect of Rogers's psychology. Recall such a statement as this: "I shall assume that the client experiences himself as being fully received." This "being fully received" by the therapist takes the place of being so accepted by God. But Rogers leaves undeveloped the important ways in which it is impossible for any human being ever fully or absolutely to receive another.

Again, Rogers's key concept of "unconditional self-regard" is simply a transformation of devout believers' conviction of God's unconditional love for them and the command that they attempt unconditional love of God in return into a full-fledged self-devotion. Rogers argues that this unconditional self-regard occurs when the client "perceives himself in such a way that no self-experience can be discriminated as more or less worthy of positive regard than any other."[28] Such a statement is completely at odds with the Christian doctrine of original sin (indeed,

26. Carl R. Rogers, *Freedom to Learn* (Columbus: Merrill, 1969).

27. Carl R. Rogers, *Client-Centered Therapy* (Boston: Houghton-Mifflin, 1951), p. 386.

28. Carl R. Rogers, "A Theory of Therapy, Personality, and Interpersonal Relationships as Developed in the Client-Centered Framework," in *Psychology: A Study of a Science,* ed. Sigmund Koch, vol. 3 (New York: McGraw-Hill, 1959), p. 209.

it compares badly even with the common human notion of moral failure), and it is still more critically in conflict with the doctrine of God's judgment. In a similar vein, Rogers advocates that the "individual, in effect, becomes his own significant social other" and "*experiences* himself as the *locus of evaluation*."[29]

The self-love advocated in Rogers's theory works itself out in the very process of client-centered therapy. This therapy technique consists in large part of reflecting back to the patient his or her own feelings, combined with the therapist's support, but without any direct advice. In its extreme form, no longer advocated by Rogers, the therapy is limited entirely to paraphrases of the patient's feelings plus general comments of empathetic support. The key word for understanding this procedure is *reflection*. The therapist is like a mirror, reflecting the patient's emotional states back to him or her.

In a most uncanny fashion, this reflective or client-centered technique recreates for the patient the conditions that long ago were powerfully described in the classical myth of Narcissus. Surrounded by the almost imperceptible therapist-manipulated mirror, the patient is forced into at least a short-term case of narcissism. After all, what else is there to fall in love with? For, in spite of self-theory's idealistic goal of trying to develop an honest self-evaluation, the theoretical principles of Rogers, unrestrained by sensible limits and moral responsibility, allow or even encourage the patient to slide into a self-gratifying, narcissistic world.

No doubt there are some young people for whom the Rogerian self-therapy is a genuine constructive experience — for example, those reared by overly moralistic, overly critical, rigidly authoritarian parents. (I have been told that such families still exist, though I do not know any. I assume they must be close to extinction.) The great irony is that recent generations, which have so enthusiastically embraced antiauthoritarian selfism, have probably grown up with the least authoritarian parents in history.

29. Rogers, "A Theory of Therapy," pp. 209, 216.

9. Psychology and the New Age Movement

References to the "New Age" are common, and most people know that the term refers to some sort of new mentality of a religious or spiritual character. There have been several critiques of the New Age movement from a Christian perspective.[1] But apparently there have been no analyses or critiques of New Age from a psychological perspective, nor have the psychological roots of New Age been articulated or explored. This chapter provides an introduction to the social and psychological origins of the New Age movement, followed by a critique of its basic positions from a psychological perspective.

The proponents of New Age spirituality commonly present their position as a radically new worldview. In particular, they reject old cultural paradigms based upon science, secular philosophy, and traditional religion; these are all seen to have "failed," to be part of the problem and not of the solution. The proponents of New Age believe that they have been empowered to initiate a "millennium of light"[2] that will redeem society from

---

1. See, e.g., Russell Chandler, *Understanding the New Age* (Dallas: Word, 1988); Douglas Groothuis, *Unmasking the New Age* (Downers Grove, IL: InterVarsity, 1986); Groothuis, *Confronting the New Age* (Downers Grove, IL: InterVarsity, 1988); Groothuis, *Revealing the New Age Jesus* (Downers Grove, IL: InterVarsity, 1990); Mitch Pacwa, *Catholics and the New Age* (Ann Arbor: Servant, 1992).

2. Marilyn Ferguson, *The Aquarian Conspiracy* (Los Angeles: Tarcher, 1980).

This chapter is based on an article by Paul C. Vitz and Deidre Modesti entitled "Social and Psychological Origins of New Age Spirituality," *Psychology and Christianity* 12 (1993): 47-57.

essentially the same. For them, Jesus, Buddha, Krishna, and others all taught and experienced the same cosmic oneness. This is what was meant by "Christ-consciousness" in the quotation given earlier. Obviously, again, New Age and Christianity are in serious theological conflict.

6. Cosmic evolutionary optimism is called for. New Age assumes that humanity, because of its newfound God-consciousness, is on an evolutionary trajectory. Humanity is at the verge of a great transformation that will usher in a new era of peace, unity, and bliss. We will become a suprahuman species. Again, Christian teaching stands in stark contrast to this sort of earthly beatific vision.

7. A final important characteristic of New Age thought is its frequent rejection of reason as "left-brain" thinking, as part of the old paradigm, in contrast to the New Age emphasis on "right-brain" mental life, such as mysticism.[10]

The relative clarity of these seven very general characteristics, however, is masked by an ambiguous hodgepodge of particulars. New Agers will include bits and pieces of all the major religions — as well as a good many other things. Russell Chandler points out: "For all its faddishness . . . the New Age is hard to define; its boundaries are fuzzy. It's a shifting kaleidoscope of 'beliefs, fads and rituals.'"[11] Parts of Buddhism, Hinduism, Sufi mysticism, and Christianity are all represented in the general eclectic New Age soup. The blends of elements of various Eastern religions would certainly offend serious practitioners of any of them. This smorgasbord of religion seems to be peculiarly American and supported by the social, ethnic, and religious pluralism of American society. Each New Ager seems to revel in picking out those components of the world's religions that he or she finds appealing. In addition to Eastern religions, another major source is primitive religion: shamanism, witchcraft, druidism, earth motherhood, ancient Egyptian religions such as the cult of Isis, etc. In many respects, the widespread Satanic cults are part of the penumbra of the New Age: an expression of their ecumenical cult of the world of spirits. In spite of the emphasis on the positive within New Age, their abandonment of dichotomy makes it impossible for them to reject the dark side of the new spirituality.

10. I owe the emphasis on this point to Mitch Pacwa (personal communication, 1992).

11. Chandler, *Understanding the New Age*, p. 17.

SOCIAL AND ECONOMIC
SUPPORT FOR NEW AGE

A number of relatively clear social and economic factors support and reinforce New Age spirituality. As already mentioned, the heterogeneity of American culture, with its increasingly complex mosaic of different religions and cultures, is a social-structural analogue to the intellectual world of New Age. Just as the act of rejecting a person because of his or her beliefs is considered antisocial and undemocratic, so also to reject religious or spiritual understandings is interpreted in the same way. Everyone and all philosophies are equally valid and admirable. Just as our social life is made up of particular individuals whom we personally like from many different ethnic and religious groups, so, by analogy, our faith can be put together in the same way. To be a seriously committed Christian is seen as an expression of social intolerance and a kind of bigotry. When tolerance is the primary accepted social virtue, commitment to a particular faith is viewed as fundamentally antisocial and even threatening.

A not insignificant contributor to New Age popularity has been the general international mentality of so many upper-middle-class Americans. The members of this governing class have traveled frequently in other countries, often on other continents; they think of themselves as citizens of the world; they often have links to the new international business community; they worry about Brazilian rain forests, the destruction of the African elephant, and the melting of the arctic ice cap. New Agers are often active supporters of world government and the still vague New World Order. In short, they see themselves as elite members of the global village. It is therefore not surprising that their religion should be devoted to cosmic consciousness based upon worldwide networks aimed at bringing the New Age of peace, light, and often ecological integrity.

Another social support for New Age has been the theological collapse of much of "mainline" Protestantism. As liberal Protestantism declined as a living reality, it left an enormous spiritual vacuum. In many instances, these spiritual needs have been filled by the apparent sophistication and novelty of New Age messages. In particular, the emphasis on spiritual experiences has contrasted very strongly with the dryness found in much of liberal Protestantism.

A similar group is composed of Catholics and former Catholics, large numbers of whom are New Agers, or at least fellow travelers. Such people have often found orthodox Catholicism to be too closely associated with embarrassing ethnic and rigid specificities, or with a lower social class than that to which they have arrived. Being vaguely aware of the importance of mystics in the Catholic tradition, they frequently use mysticism as a bridge from orthodoxy to the New Age. The evolutionary and spiritual model of Teilhard de Chardin[12] and especially Fr. Matthew Fox, with his creation spirituality, are good examples of the phenomenon. Fox's approach often merges with such New Age themes as "Channeling, Reincarnation, Witchcraft, Neopaganism and the Occult."[13]

A big contributor to the New Age culture — the immediate origins of which go back into the 1960s — has been the widespread use of drugs. The drug culture in America has been commonly associated with many New Age classics. The use of drugs in many primitive religions became well known, and significant numbers of influential Americans began to explore the link between drug use and religious experience. The recourse to drugs by shamans and Native American medicine men became a topic of interest, and many experimented with a combination of drugs and primitive ritual.

Another feature of American society supporting the New Age is our country's rootlessness — and in particular, the collapse of our historical and cultural traditions in the past thirty years. Nowhere has this rootlessness been more prevalent than in California, the acknowledged geographical center and source of the New Age. It is the home of everything from the Esalen Institute to Shirley MacLaine to Matthew Fox. As our links to the past have withered, along with fading traditions and traditional morals, New Age, with its sophisticated sampling of the "best" of the world's religions and its celebration of the future as well as its open-ended present, has arrived to take the place of our religious and cultural memory.

The American consumer society fully supports the New Age approach to religion, as it is predicated on the assumption that all choices are made on the basis of personal preference from the array provided in the marketplace. The "divine right" of the consumer to choose as he or she pleases has become so common an idea that it operates in millions of Americans like an unconscious tropism.

Closely related to the consumer support for New Age mentality is

12. See Wolfgang Smith, *Teilhardism and the New Religion* (Rockford, IL: TAN, 1988).
13. See Weinandy, "Review of Groothuis."

the economic prosperity of American society. Much of the New Age optimism and belief in change as evolution — that is, progress — is derived from the experience of some fifty years or more of steady economic improvement for so many Americans. These economic and above all consumer aspects of our society provide the link between a social and a psychological explanation of New Age popularity.

PSYCHOLOGICAL ORIGINS OF NEW AGE

New Age has many ancestors; it is not as though psychology created it, like Athena emerging full-grown from the brow of Zeus. But psychology was one of the major intellectual and social forces that brought today's movement into cultural prominence. One such source of support for New Age has come from Freud and Jung, who both, in different ways, emphasized the importance of the unconscious. These psychologists created a whole climate of opinion that made the unconscious, interior world seem more real than the conscious mind, with its awareness of external reality. Thus, New Agers — prominent among them, Shirley MacLaine[14] — come into contact with their hitherto inarticulate inner "Higher Self," who teaches them the truth about life and about themselves.

However, the primary psychological source for New Age was humanistic psychology, and most especially Abraham Maslow, clearly a key force in conceptualizing humanistic psychology. Carl Rogers, the major co-creator of humanistic psychology along with Maslow, was primarily focused on therapeutic techniques; it was his general client-centered interpretation of the counseling setting that had the greatest effects. Thus Rogers had great impact on the practice of psychotherapy and counseling, but he had less influence on theoretical interpretations of personality as generally conceived. Nevertheless, Rogers was quite sympathetic, near the end of his life, to New Age concepts.[15]

Eric Fromm's contributions to humanistic psychology were significant but primarily cultural and social; his work made relatively little direct contact with the life of individuals. Abraham Maslow was primarily

14. Shirley MacLaine, *Going Within: A Guide for Inner Transformation* (New York: Bantam, 1989), chap. 5.
15. Carl R. Rogers, *A Way of Being* (Boston: Houghton Mifflin, 1980).

a personality theorist; he had relatively little to say about or contribute to the actual process of therapy. Maslow's major contribution was probably his book *Motivation and Personality*,[16] and the title identifies its central concern. Maslow's most basic notion was his well-known hierarchy of human needs. At the highest level of this hierarchy of needs, which supposedly underlies the personality development of all human beings, is Maslow's most famous concept: the presumed need for self-actualization. At the top of self-actualization Maslow placed the "peak experience." This peak experience is a transcendent experience of oneness and wholeness and unity with the cosmos, and Maslow explicitly states that this experience is a natural — not a supernatural — phenomenon. He assumes that religious figures often reached this stage, but after coming out of the peak experience they or their fellow religionists made the mistake of interpreting it in terms of the content of the religion that their culture had given them. Thus this peak experience is for Maslow a purely natural, albeit a transcendent, phenomenon.[17] Near the end of his life, Maslow became more and more interested in the transcendent experience, and he was among the most important founders of a new journal called *The Journal of Transpersonal Psychology (JTP)*, which began publishing in 1969. By this time in his life Maslow was living in California and had links to the Esalen Institute. The new *JTP* was first announced by Maslow at a Unitarian Church in California.[18] A quick look at the reference sections of articles in the *JTP* makes clear that Maslow is a major founding author and is clearly the most frequently cited psychologist.

The *JTP* focuses on transcendent experience and its implications for personal life and growth. It makes almost no pretense to being part of traditional scientific psychology; even the reasonably rigorous thinking of psychoanalysts and cognitive and behavioral psychologists is, if not disdained, at least ignored in the great majority of *JTP* articles. Clearly, the break between psychology and the transcendent — and in many cases, spirituality — was made in *JTP*. This is not to say that the

16. Abraham Maslow, *Motivation and Personality* (1954; 2nd ed. New York: Harper & Row, 1970).

17. Abraham Maslow, *Religions, Values and Peak Experiences* (Columbus: Ohio State University Press, 1954), pp. 26-27.

18. See A. J. Sutich, "Some Considerations Regarding Transpersonal Psychology," *Journal of Transpersonal Psychology* 1 (1969): 11-20.

articles about spiritual experience found there are without scholarly merit. The point is that in moving to the transcendent these articles moved into an entirely new realm of intellectual discourse, a realm that leaves the psychological origin of the movement behind. But humanistic psychology, via Maslow, was their launching pad.

The explicit link between transpersonal psychology and New Age became visible in 1978 when the *JTP* sponsored a conference on "Consciousness and the Cosmos." Held in California, this conference included such important New Age figures as Fritjof Capra.[19]

Many of the transpersonal psychologists still seem to assume that transcendent or spiritual experience is a special kind of natural phenomenon. These writers interpret the transcendent experience as a phenomenon that can be brought about by systematic study and practice. For example, mental exercises that separate or detach the person from the world of perception, thought, and memory facilitate this experience of a liberated consciousness. They understand the traditional religious disciplines, both physical (e.g., fasting, yoga) and mental (e.g., meditation, spiritual reading, Buddhist koans), as natural practices that facilitate mental detachment to the point where one can eventually have a peak, or transcendent, spiritual high. In this kind of experience it is assumed that you are completely out of touch with all earthly reality and with your past experiences of it. Other *JTP* authors assume that you are also in touch with the divine, in some sense of that word — for example, a world life force, a divine reality within yourself, the divine reality that permeates the entire cosmos and is in all things (i.e., pantheistic monism), etc.

In short, in the 1970s and 1980s the *JTP* served to legitimatize the topics of the transcendent or spiritual for a large group of psychologists and other intellectuals who had been raised in a skeptical, rationalistic, and materialistic academic framework. In this journal, and in the meetings of transpersonal psychologists, they found intellectual evidence and social support with which to reject the worldviews of the behaviorists, the Freudians, and even many of the more empirically oriented humanistic psychologists. The transpersonal psychologists needed ways to exorcise the ghosts of nineteenth-century materialist philosophers that had so long dominated psychology and all social science, disciplines that needed materialist and positivist philosophy to support their claims to

19. Fritjof Capra, *The Tao of Physics* (Suffolk, England: Chaucer, 1975).

scientific legitimacy. Many humanistic psychologists, or psychologists of similar type, wrote for *JTP* and elsewhere on spiritual topics. For example, Charles T. Tart, a Stanford Ph.D., edited a book called *Transpersonal Psychologies*,[20] contributors to which included several psychologists deeply involved in "mystical" experience, as well as philosophers and explicitly religious writers.

One of the major early New Age figures is known as Ram Dass; his original name was Richard Alpert. Like Tart, he received his Ph.D. in psychology from Stanford. In the early 1960s he was closely connected with Timothy Leary, a Ph.D. in psychology from the University of California at Berkeley. They both got jobs as psychologists at Harvard University. To Harvard they brought LSD and other mind-expanding early forms of New Age thinking. Ram Dass (Alpert) acknowledges that his drug experiences initiated his spiritual journeys. After being fired from Harvard, Alpert began long visits to India and turned to Eastern religion in a very dramatic way, eventually changing his name to Ram Dass. He is still well known, although he is more systematic than many New Age figures.[21]

The most historically important psychologist with major New Age links is Carl Jung. In many respects Jung was a pioneer humanistic psychologist in that his concept of self-realization was extremely similar to Maslow's self-actualization — except that he developed and published the idea years earlier. But Jung's humanistic notions were not especially appreciated by the American humanistic psychologists for reasons that are not clear. On the other hand, Jung's involvement in mythology, the occult, and religion as an expression of the individual's unconscious has had considerable vogue in transpersonal psychology and in parts of New Age spirituality. Apparently Jung's concern with interpreting dreams and the symbols found in world mythology, as well as his personal and intellectual involvement in the occult, has contributed to his New Age popularity. Jung was long known to have been, in his later writings, sympathetic to religion, but his sympathy was not with any form of orthodox or traditional faith. Rather, his sympathy was with a highly personalistic and subjective understanding of religious life.

20. Charles T. Tart, ed., *Transpersonal Psychologies* (New York: Harper & Row, 1975).
21. Ram Dass, *Journeys of Awakening* (New York: Bantam, 1990). Some biographical information is based on my personal acquaintance with Alpert during the period 1957 to 1962.

NEW AGE AS A NEW GNOSTICISM

A few writers, including New Age figures such as Ferguson, have pointed out the similarities between New Age systems and Gnosticism.[22] Gnosticism arose in the Hellenistic period, apparently in the century or two before the birth of Christ. At the time of early Christianity there were many Gnostic sects, and in spite of the important differences between them they shared a number of features. First, as the name "gnostic" (or "knower") implies, these systems proposed knowledge as the key to the meaning of life. In a sense, for all Gnostics, salvation comes through knowledge. Roughly two thousand years ago the kind of knowledge emphasized was philosophical or spiritual, usually of an esoteric (i.e., secret) kind. These sects combined various ingredients taken from a wide assortment of ancient religious and philosophical sources. Some Gnostics borrowed concepts or practices from Greek philosophy (such as Platonism); others were influenced by Indian religious ideas, others by Egyptian religion, and some by Jewish religious sources as well.

With the rise of Christianity, there were a number of Christian Gnostic groups. This is not the place to go into the history of Gnosticism, which is both extremely complex and a source of considerable scholarly controversy. Nevertheless, there is consensus on the religious syncretism and esoteric nature of Gnosticism. New Age systems can be clearly seen as a recrudescence of Gnosticism, in a form quite similar to its ancient manifestations. Once again we have wide variations in general concepts, with only loose ties to particular practice. We again have syncretism, the mixing of Hindu, Buddhist, and Christian elements, with Native American features occasionally thrown in. Again we have a strong resistance to fixed doctrines or dogmas and a central belief that it is in knowing that we reach salvation. That is, we are saved, from whatever is the worst that can happen to us, by knowledge. In New Age this knowledge is often self-knowledge or knowledge about how to let go of or escape the self. (For a good discussion of the Gnostic movement in the West, with special reference to neopaganism in the modern period, see Thomas Molnar's analysis.)[23]

It is also relevant that the social conditions of the ancient Greco-Roman world, especially in the eastern Mediterranean, are similar to

22. Ferguson, *The Aquarian Conspiracy*, e.g., p. 46.
23. Thomas Molnar, *The Pagan Temptation* (Grand Rapids: Eerdmans, 1987).

those in which the New Age flourishes today. Los Angeles is a new Alexandria: rich, pleasure-loving, a crossroad of cultures and religious traditions. In Southern California, Eastern religions are clearly influential, not only because of the many Anglo-American Californians involved in Buddhism and Hinduism, but also because the Orient itself is a major commercial and cultural presence. In addition, of course, there are now millions of persons of Asian descent living in California. Furthermore, there are also considerable numbers of Muslims in the Los Angeles area, who add their spiritual traditions, such as Sufism, and implicitly undermine any Christian or other religious claim to a distinctive religious authority. Jewish elements are mixed in as well, adding yet another religious flavor to the syncretic stew. The conditions that are found on a rather large scale in California are increasingly found, although sometimes on a small scale, throughout the Western world. Therefore the appeal of New Age would appear to have a growing future, since the social conditions that favor it are becoming increasingly common and widespread.

As already noted, one of the characteristics of the New Age mentality is a certain kind of optimism. This optimism is based upon the possibility of reaching a spiritual state of transcendence resulting in inner peace, and on the belief that the New Age movement itself is an evolutionary wave that will crest by bringing its answers to the problems of the world. Lurking behind this optimism, however, seems to be a form of pessimism that has not yet been articulated within the movement. The movement from psychology to spirituality is itself indicative of such pessimism. After all, the humanistic psychologists proposed that the meaning of life could be found in this world in the form of psychological self-knowledge and psychological processes of self-expression. The movement to the New Age, however, represents a radical shift in the locus of salvation or happiness. It is as though New Agers have given up on psychology and are pessimistic about any form of knowledge linked to this world. Implicit in the New Age is the idea that it is only in escape from this world that happiness or peace can be found. In some respects, of course, the same charge could be made (and has been made) about Christianity, with its focus on heaven. But it is worth remembering that Jesus made it very clear that the door to heaven was open to those who kept his commandments in this world. Furthermore, the created world, including the human body, is seen as good, despite the impact of sin. Thus the tests of the Christian life are both detachment from and action in this world: love of God and love of neighbor. The New Age, however, knows no law of love. In part this is because it knows no laws at all, since laws imply a law-giver, and in part it is the result of the great focus on subjective experience, which is the fundamental reality. Since the new reality is the result of spiritual practices or enlightenment, any failures or tragedies in one's life or in others' lives are ultimately the individual's responsibility. The poor, therefore, are seen as responsible for their own condition, and not as fellow humans to whom we owe love.

New Age pessimism also follows from its rejection of the external world of reality, including our physical body. New Agers reject the body and the sexual character of our identity by emphasizing androgyny. The physical world is often interpreted as essentially an illusion. Bodies are arbitrary and can be manipulated at will. Moreover, in an earlier life one had a different body, and one may have other quite different bodies in the future.

Finally, to the extent that America's New Age optimism is based on our prosperity and wealth, its theoretical pessimism is likely to surface quite strongly in a period of economic stagnation, and even more in response to a serious decline in economic well-being.

In any case, there is every reason to expect New Age religious syncretism to continue to grow and to challenge Christianity — along with other traditional religions. And it is likely that, as time goes on, its underlying pessimism about this world will express itself with increasing clarity.

NEW AGE SPIRITUALITY: FROM
PSYCHOLOGICAL TO SPIRITUAL SELF-WORSHIP

Social psychology in recent years has very thoroughly documented the human tendency to narcissistic self-understanding with its research on what is called the "self-serving bias." For example, as already noted, there is a reliable tendency for people to accept responsibility for their successes and to attribute failure to the environment or to other causes outside of their control; we also have a tendency to see ourselves as above average on most salient personal dimensions.[24]

24. For this literature, see D. T. Miller and M. Ross, "Self-serving Biases in the Attribution of Causality: Fact or Fiction," *Psychological Bulletin* 82 (1975): 213-25; D. T. Miller and C. A. Porter, "Errors and Biases in the Attribution Process," in *Socio-personal*

In any case, it is the thesis of this book that the humanistic model of human behavior is fundamentally narcissistic, and that this has resulted in its widespread appeal in our culture. The consumer economy, combined with natural human pride (narcissism), has created a psychology that is focused on the individual's glorification of his or her own self.

Perhaps it should be made clear that by the word *narcissism* I do not mean the seriously disturbed narcissistic personality, but rather a kind of general, social narcissism — what Adler might have called a "style of life" narcissism. Thus today's socially narcissistic person would be predicted to have a greater likelihood of divorce, a tendency to spend less time with spouse and children and more time on self, and a marked involvement in consumer goods and activities. One would also predict a low commitment to community and to charity.

The present interpretation of how psychological self-worship, deriving from humanistic psychology, transformed itself into spiritual self-worship in the American context is as follows. The immense popularity of humanistic psychology and its derivatives in the United States in the 1950s, 1960s, and 1970s led to large-scale disappointment with the promises these theories made. With self-actualization of the individual came two painful realities. First, such motivation often resulted in the breakdown of interpersonal relations (e.g., divorce and other estrangements). Second, as people aged, they realized that many of the things thought necessary for self-actualization would not be attainable in their lives. Besides interpersonal disasters, there were career failures, serious health problems, and many other disappointments. The discrepancy between the promised "high" of the Maslovian self-actualization or Jungian individuation and the reality of their lives created a vast disappointment and "credibility gap." The belief that psychology could make you happy, that it was the answer, began to fade.

Too many tried self-psychology and found it wanting. Psychology may have helped, briefly, but life remained painful and difficult. Countless Americans were discovering the general truth in Freud's comment about psychoanalytic psychotherapy, that the best it could do was to return the patient to the normal level of human misery. But people still

Inference in Clinical Psychology, ed. L. Abramson (New York: Guilford, 1988), pp. 3-29. See also M. Zuckerman, "Attribution of Success and Failure Revisited, or: The Motivational Bias Is Alive and Well in Attribution Theory," *Journal of Personality* 47 (1979): 245-87; David G. Myers, *Social Psychology* (New York: McGraw-Hill, 1990).

sought "true" happiness or complete inner peace or some justifying internal positive state. Therefore they turned to spiritual experience and a spiritual understanding of their condition. In general, however, they did not turn to traditional religions — or at least large numbers did not. I am arguing here that they did not turn to traditional religions because of the restraints on narcissism, especially moral restraints, which almost every major religion requires. The freedom to "have it your way" both in the moral and in the intellectual realm is central to the appeal of New Age spirituality. Thus the thesis proposed here is that New Age spirituality is the transformation of psychological narcissism into spiritual narcissism.

The seven points enumerated earlier in this chapter all strongly support this interpretation of New Age. The idea that each person is divine (point 3) directly encourages self-worship. The notions that all is one, all is God, and all religions are one (points 1, 2, and 5) also support narcissism by suspending distinctions between good and evil and between true and false. This allows religion, morality, and truth to be self-defined. All particular laws, all struggles with internal sin or pride are ultimately meaningless if distinctions and polarities collapse into one vast undifferentiated category. Point 7 — the rejection of reason — means that the New Ager is exempt from criticism. This exemption isolates the narcissist in his or her own self-confirming world, since criticism requires reason — words, speech, and writing. Point 4, the need for a change of consciousness, assumes that each person is the source of this change and therefore of his or her own salvation. Point 6, which calls for "cosmic evolutionary optimism," reinforces and justifies the whole narcissistic system.

In short, we have gone from self-actualization, with its support in our self-indulgent consumer economy, to New Age consumer spirituality, without losing a beat. One of the popular advocates of New Age, Hollywood's Shirley MacLaine, sums up all of this in her statement: "Each soul is its own god. You must never worship anyone or anything other than self. For *you* are God. To love self is to love God."[25] In this sense, New Age is as old as Adam and Eve, who also gave in to the ultimate (as well as the original) narcissistic act, true self-worship: "You shall be as gods."

25. Shirley MacLaine, *Dancing in the Light* (New York: Bantam, 1983), p. 358.

10. A Christian Critique

SELFISM AS IDOLATRY

It should be obvious — though it has apparently not been so to many — that the relentless and single-minded search for and glorification of the self is at direct cross-purposes with the Christian injunction to lose the self. Certainly Jesus Christ neither lived nor advocated a life that would qualify by today's standards as "self-actualized." For the Christian, the self is the problem, not the potential paradise. Understanding this problem involves an awareness of sin, especially the sin of pride; correcting this condition requires the practice of such unself-actualized states as contrition and penitence, humility, obedience, and trust in God.

Some comments from Paul Ramsey's *Basic Christian Ethics* are appropriate here.

> The first assertion Christian ethics makes about man is that he was created for personal existence within the image of God, and that Jesus Christ most perfectly reveals this image. The second assertion is that man is sinful. So fundamental is this doctrine in Christian thought that it cannot be overlooked. Indeed, many theologians regard it as basic equally with the first for any full understanding of man in the light of God. This has been the view not only of the more "pessimistic" thinkers; it was the view also of John Wesley, whose emphasis upon "going on to perfection" is well known.[1]

The Christian position is clear that sin is not exclusively or primarily something in society. It is something that all humans do, and do as a

1. Paul Ramsey, *Basic Christian Ethics* (New York: Scribners, 1950), p. 284.

willed act, not merely as the consequence of outside influences on them. The locus of sin, therefore, is in the will of each of us. This central Christian doctrine has been under relentless attack for many years by almost all advocates of social science, from traditional economics and sociology to Socialism and Communism. Ordinary Christians, un-defended by their own theologians, have often succumbed to the position that evil lies only or primarily in society. As a consequence, a central foundation of their doctrinal system has been undermined. A powerful and imaginative attack on the social science position comes from the Russian Christian Aleksandr Solzhenitsyn:

> Gradually it was disclosed to me that the line separating good and evil passes not through states, nor between classes, nor between political parties either — but right through every human heart. . . .
>
> Since then I have come to understand the truth of all the religions of the world: they struggle with the *evil inside a human being* (inside every human being). It is impossible to expel evil from the world in its entirety, but it is possible to constrict it within each person.
>
> And since that time I have come to understand the falsehood of all revolutions in history: they destroy only *those carriers* of evil contem-porary with them (and also out of haste, to discriminate the carriers of good as well). And they then take to themselves as their heritage the actual evil itself, magnified still more.[2]

In spite of the antireligious prejudice of modern psychology, a few prominent psychologists appreciate the psychological necessity of ac-cepting sin. One is O. Hobart Mowrer, who has written as follows:

> For several decades we psychologists looked upon the whole matter of sin and moral accountability as a great incubus and acclaimed our liberation from it as epoch-making. But at length we have discovered that to be "free" in this sense, i.e., to have the excuse of being "sick" rather than sinful, is to court the danger of also becoming lost. This danger is, I believe, betokened by the widespread interest in Existen-tialism which we are presently witnessing. In becoming amoral, ethically

2. Aleksandr I. Solzhenitsyn, *The Gulag Archepelago*, trans. T. P. Whitney, vols. 3-4 (New York: Harper & Row, 1974-78), pp. 615-16. See also Leonard Shapiro, "Disturbing, Fanatical, and Heroic," *New York Review of Books*, 13 Nov. 1975, p. 10; and Aleksandr I. Solzhenitsyn et al., *From Under the Rubble*, trans. A. M. Brook (Boston: Little Brown, 1975), esp. the essay by "A.B."

neutral, and "free," we have cut the very roots of our being; lost our deepest sense of self-hood and identity; and with neurotics themselves, find ourselves asking: "who *am* I?"[3]

The great benefit of the doctrine of sin is that it reintroduces responsibility for our own behavior, responsibility for changing, as well as giving meaning to our condition. Mowrer describes these benefits from the acceptance of sin:

> Just so long as a person lives under the shadow of real, unacknowledged, and unexpiated guilt, he *cannot* (if he has any character at all) "accept himself"; and all *our* efforts to reassure and accept him will avail nothing. He will continue to hate himself and to suffer the inevitable consequences of self-hatred. But the moment he (with or without "assistance") begins to accept his guilt and sinfulness, the possibility of radical reformation opens up; and with this, the individual may legitimately, though not without pain and effort, pass from deep, pervasive self-rejection and self-torture to a new freedom, of self-respect and peace.[4]

The problems posed by humanistic selfism are not new to Christianity; indeed, they can be traced back to early conflicts with Stoicism and other sophisticated Greco-Roman philosophical and ethical systems. To worship one's self (in self-realization) or to worship all humanity is, in Christian terms, simple idolatry operating from the usual motive of unconscious egotism. Unconscious or disguised self-love has long been recognized as the source of idolatry. Otto Baab, in his study of Old Testament theology, describes it thus:

> Idolatry is well understood in the Bible as differing from the pure worship of Israel's God in the fact of its personification and objectification of the human will in contrast with the superhuman transcendence of the true God. When an idol is worshipped, man is worshipping himself, his desires, his purposes and his will. . . . As a consequence of this type of idolatry man was outrageously guilty of giving himself the status of God and of exalting his own will as of supreme worth.[5]

3. O. Hobart Mowrer, "Sin, the Lesser of Two Evils," *American Psychologist* 15 (1960): 303.

4. Mowrer, "Sin," p. 304.

5. Otto Baab, *The Theology of the Old Testament* (New York: Abingdon/Cokesbury, 1949), pp. 105, 110; quoted by Ramsey, *Basic Christian Ethics,* p. 298.

Such an analysis makes it clear that in religious terms selfist humanism is just another example of idolatrous narcissism.

After the establishment of Christianity, the worship of the self continued as a many-faceted heresy. Besides Gnosticism, elements of modern selfism are found in the medieval sect called the Brethren of the Free Spirit and in many other sects.[6] The present form of selfism also contains strong Pelagian strands. Pelagius, a fourth-century theologian from Britain, opposed the doctrine of original sin and argued that humans are capable of living a perfect and sinless life, thus downgrading the importance of God's grace.[7] Evans in a scholarly treatment points out that Pelagius's position was not as extreme as his critics have often portrayed it.[8] Pelagius remained a Christian theologian, and even so vigorous an opponent of his as St. Augustine acknowledged him to be a "saintly man." But a strong element in his theology might, under its traditional and rather extreme interpretation, be viewed as akin to humanist selfism. So it has been accepted by Fromm, who cites Pelagius as an ally and as a representative of what he calls "humanistic" religion, in contrast to the "authoritarian" religion typified by Augustine. Evans, however, notes that Fromm's categories of "humanistic"

6. See Paul Zweig, *The Heresy of Self-Love* (New York: Harper & Row, 1968).

7. The humanist aspect of Pelagius's theology is sometimes said to be temperamentally natural to the English and by extension to Americans. There may be some small grain of truth here, but the relative quiescence of Pelagianism in England for more than a thousand years after his death raises questions for such an interpretation. A more probable explanation would involve the unusual economic and social factors present in England in the later fourth century, the formative time for Pelagius's thinking. The first was a preceding period of nearly two hundred years of increasing economic prosperity — roughly from the second century to the end of the fourth century. This was the British-Roman period of country villas and baths. The second condition was the probable effect of the combined Roman and Christian culture — both powerful and civilizing imports to a previously pagan and rather primitive Britain. Such a qualitatively new and superior culture, combined with a substantial long-term increase in wealth, could easily have created the belief in Britain and in some other parts of the Roman Empire that a new era had dawned and the old laws of human nature and history no longer operated. Shortly after the death of Pelagius, around 431, Britain relapsed into wars, social breakdown, and barbarism — all of which may have provided more effective anti-Pelagian "arguments" than those of St. Augustine or St. Jerome. There is in this example an obvious historical similarity to America's two hundred years of greatly increasing wealth, combined with the belief that science has ushered in a new condition of progress in which the old understanding of human nature and its limits is no longer relevant.

8. On Pelagius, see Robert F. Evans, *Pelagius: Inquiries and Reappraisals* (New York: Seabury, 1968).

and "authoritarian" religion do not fit the theologies of either Pelagius or Augustine. (This is just one example of how Fromm's bias in his writings concerning Christianity leads him to misread Christian theology and faith.)[9]

Furthermore, with respect to the problem of authoritarianism, it should be noted that Christians from the beginning have been aware of the problems of excessive institutionalized authority and the dangers of bad faith that it can create. Over a two-thousand-year period the Christian response has been recurring spiritual revival and renewal. While there is a legitimate dichotomy between frozen, institutionalized, or severely formalized religion and a living, spiritual faith, authority per se operates in both types of religion. Today's bureaucratized, secularized, and highly humanized Christianity provides an example of an intellectualized dead faith. Much of this Christianity has been drained of its vitality by an over-generalized psychology, of which an obvious example is the very humanist selfism Fromm espouses, which has become increasingly authoritative.

Like all popular heresy, selfism has some positive and appealing properties. That you should look out for yourself is nice (and useful) to hear; that you should try to be positive toward others is also nice and somewhat familiar. What is excluded is the spiritual life of prayer, meditation, and worship — the essential vertical dimension of Christianity, the relation to God. Selfism is an example of a horizontal heresy, with its emphasis only on the present and on self-centered ethics.

THE PROBLEM OF DEPRESSION

Some psychologists have justified self-theory by pointing out the large number of people who suffer from depression and associated negative thoughts about themselves. The idea is that emphasizing self-love will somehow correct this obviously disturbing and unfortunate form of suffering. The first point to make here is that depression is not a simple phenomenon; there are different kinds of depression with different kinds of causes. Many depressions have biological origins and require some

9. See, e.g., Erich Fromm, *Psychoanalysis and Religion* (New Haven: Yale University Press, 1950), pp. 34 and 49.

kind of medication — an approach to depression commonly overlooked by self-theorists, at the expense of many of their clients.

Depression can have psychological origins, but in these cases it is typically a disguised form of self-worship. This suggestion might, at first, appear surprising, but the rationale is simple: depression and negative thoughts about oneself are often the result of aggression turned against the self, an aggression or self-hatred that occurs when one fails to meet one's own high standards for success. People get depressed because they fail to get married, to get promoted, to be made a partner, to become rich, to be recognized as an artist, and so forth. An enormous amount of pride lurks behind our attachment to the standards we fail to live up to. That is, optimistic self-confidence and pessimistic depression often result from the self taking on the prerogatives of creating the standards of its own worth. This narcissistic self then judges how well one meets these standards. When we fail to meet them, it is our own self that condemns us. In Christian terms, however, one's worth comes from God, not from our self-selected standards. Furthermore, a person is not to judge himself or herself — or anyone else. Judgment belongs to God, and to judge oneself is to take God's place. (A purely secular psychological theory of this kind of self-hatred and the problems it poses was developed by Karen Horney.)[10]

In any case, psychologically creating your own self-worth is like printing your own money — it leads to false prosperity: inflation followed by depression. Self-talk about how wonderful you are doesn't work if the next day the real situation remains the same. Like drugs, self-psychology sessions can give short-term elation, but a few hours later the elation has worn off and a depressive reaction sets in.

THE PROBLEM OF THE HUMAN DOORMAT

Psychologists have also advocated many of the self-psychology principles in response to people — often women — who suffer from exploitive relationships. The basic rationale is that women caught in abusive relationships lack adequate self-esteem, which has to be increased in order for them to break out of their love trap, their destructive pattern. I certainly agree that many of these relationships are destructive and

10. Karen Horney, *Neurosis and Human Growth* (New York: Norton, 1950).

that the problem is to escape from them and to avoid them in the future. My disagreement is with the common strategy for attaining these goals. The first problem, I believe, is that many of these people (they are not all women) have idolized their lover and the love relationship. And I mean *idolized* in the strong sense. It is because they worship the other person, or because they worship a love relationship, that they are in the pickle they are in. Again, a secular psychologist has identified this problem. Karen Horney refers to such interpretations of one's lover and of love as "neurotic ideals."[11] So the first issue to address is the inappropriate adoration that has been bestowed on the love object. From a Christian perspective, the second issue is almost invariably the absence of a true love of God in the person's life. By love of God I do not mean a vague affect, but rather a commitment to God's law — "If you love me, you will keep my commandments" — and the *appropriate* love of neighbor. To love God is to acquire a strong sense of one's own worth in God's eyes and real detachment from all things of this world, including love objects. One is no longer a neurotic "compliant" type. No Christian can adore, or blindly submit to, any other human being.

CHRISTIAN LOVE AND SELFIST LOVE

Christianity and selfism differ not just over the self and self-love but also over the very nature of love. To begin reflection on the Christian conception of love, recall that Christ summarized the whole law in two commands to love: "Thou shalt love the Lord thy God with all thy heart, with all thy soul, and with all thy strength" and "Thou shalt love thy neighbor as thyself." The love of God is first. It is primary, and love of neighbor stems from it. Love in these two forms is at the very center of the Christian faith. Note, too, that there is no direct command to love the self — an adequate degree of self-love being assumed natural.

    This Christian theory of love has been expressed for nearly two thousand years in what is now an enormous tradition. It shines forth in the life and death of Jesus as recorded in the four Gospels; it is disclosed in the writings of St. Paul, St. Augustine, St. Bernard, Martin Luther, the Wesleys, Tolstoy, C. S. Lewis, and many, many more; it is given con-

---

11. Horney, *Neurosis and Human Growth*; also Karen Horney, *Our Inner Conflicts* (New York: Norton, 1945).

temporary application in a wide variety of personal and institutional practices. Christian love has been shown in the early Christian communities, in the age-old and still lively monastic tradition, in the expressions of medieval and Eastern Orthodox mysticism, in the emotional caring shown by pietist groups, in Christian hospitals, missions, and the Salvation Army. The lives of St. Francis in thirteenth-century Europe, Mother Teresa in twentieth-century Calcutta, the host of saints, and countless other good, quiet Christians are such remarkable and historically unique examples of the expression of love that it should be obvious that their faith had something to do with it. It is by turns flabbergasting and disturbing that nowhere in the selfist writings about love is this large body of Christian theory and practice ever discussed.

Fromm in his well-known book *The Art of Loving* presents what he describes as "The Theory of Love." In the discussion of love of God he follows the Feuerbachian approach by assuming that "the understanding of the concept of God must . . . start with an analysis of the character structure of the person who worships God."[12] Although he is less blatantly hostile to Christianity here than in his earlier work *The Dogma of Christ,* he does conclude, by various social and vaguely historical arguments, that the God professed by Christian theology is an illusion. His discussion of love includes some citations from the Christian mystic Meister Eckhart that imply that the human person is God. But these quotations are certainly not Christian, and they seriously misrepresent Meister Eckhart's theology. Eckhart's view of self-love is quite explicit: he calls it "the root and cause of all evil, depriving us of all goodness and perfection. Therefore, if the soul is to know God it must forget and lose itself; so long as it mirrors its own image it does not see or know God."[13] There is no word about keeping the self's integrity, using the self to define what is good, or any other of the familiar selfist themes. Fromm, in addition to misrepresenting Eckhart, completely neglects the major body of Christian writing on love.

Similarly, Maslow, in his major work *Motivation and Personality,* primarily discusses love between the sexes; he has no Christian references.

12. Erich Fromm, *The Art of Loving* (New York: Harper, 1956), p. 63.

13. Quoted by Otto Karrar, ed., *Meister Eckhart Speaks* (London: Blackfriars, 1957), p. 41. See also J. M. Clark, *The Great German Mystics* (Oxford: B. Blackwell, 1949); and Etienne Gilson, *Christian Philosophy in the Middle Ages* (New York: Random House, 1955).

In some of his later writings, however, he does take seriously the mystic experience — at least a secular understanding of it.[14] But Maslow's writings contain no treatment of Christian mysticism, much less any discussion of Christian love.

Carl Rogers, in his best-known contribution to personality theory and psychotherapy, *On Becoming a Person,* has no treatment of love at all. Nor is love discussed in Rogers's book on encounter groups. Even his *Becoming Partners* has no theory of love — its emphasis is on sexual compatibility, changing roles and relationships, learning to trust the self and others, and the like. Needless to say, there is no recognition or acknowledgment of the Christian theory of love here.

As was pointed out above, it is essential in discussing Christian love to emphasize love of God — above all to emphasize that the love of God is for a Christian not primarily an intellectual dogma but an empirical fact, an overwhelming experiential reality. It is from this experienced reality that theology begins. In the final analysis, all Christian theology is a theory of love, of divine love. Those unfamiliar with or dubious about such a spiritual state can translate "the love of God" into such terms as "contemplation," "meditation," or "mystic experience." Such translations are not adequate for Christian theology, but they will suffice for the present analysis.

The Christian theoretical claim is that love of God or Christ not only justifies the love of others but also greatly facilitates it. St. Bernard's four-stage hierarchical model of the love of God is a famous twelfth-century conceptualization of the Christian's relation to the first commandment and the resulting consequences for the love of others. A brief summary of his position (from his *De diligendo Deo* or "On Loving God")[15] exemplifies the kind of literature the selfists overlook.

St. Bernard begins by saying that the wise person loves God simply because God is God, but for others amplification is needed. The first degree of love is love of the self for self, which he assumes to be natural and good, unless it runs to excess, when at this stage it should be controlled by the command to love one's neighbor as oneself. The second degree is love of God for what he gives. For Christians, the initial reason

14. See, e.g., Abraham H. Maslow, *Religions, Values, and Peak Experiences* (New York: Viking, 1970).

15. Bernard de Clairvaux, "On Loving God," trans. Robert Walton, in *The Works of Bernard of Clairvaux: Treatises II* (Washington, DC: Cistercian Publications/Consortium Press, 1974), pp. 93-132.

for loving God is that God loves them, that God has loved first. This love, expressed in the creation of the world, reaches sublime expression in the New Testament: "For God so loved the world that he gave his only Son, that whoever believes in him should not perish but have eternal life" (John 3:16). Thus, this degree is love of God for his many blessings, including solace found in times of trouble. It is through this love that the Christian first learns his or her limitations and weaknesses.

The third stage is love of God for what God is. In this stage God is loved purely for himself, because we "discover how sweet the Lord is. Tasting God's sweetness entices us more to pure love than does the urgency of our own needs." Bernard notes that a person "who feels this way will not have trouble in fulfilling the commandment to love his neighbor. He loves God truthfully and so loves what is God's. He loves purely and he does not find it hard to obey a pure commandment, purifying his heart, as it is written, in the obedience of love."[16]

Finally, Bernard describes the fourth degree, which is difficult and rare: "This love is a mountain, God's towering peak. Truly indeed, it is the fat, fertile mountain. . . . I would say that man is blessed and holy to whom it is given to experience something of this sort, so rare in life, even if it be but once and for the space of a moment. To lose yourself, as if you no longer existed, to cease completely to experience yourself, to reduce yourself to nothing is not a human sentiment but a divine experience."[17]

The alignment of one's will with that of God in this fourth stage is described by St. Bernard thus:

> Just as red, molten iron becomes so much like fire it seems to lose its primary state; just as the air on a sunny day seems transformed into sunshine instead of being lit up; so it is necessary for the saints that all human feelings melt in a mysterious way and flow into the will of God. Otherwise, how will God be all in all if something human survives in man? No doubt, the substance remains though under another form, another glory, another power.[18]

This final degree allows the love of oneself "for God's sake" — that is, we love ourselves as God loves us.

16. Bernard, "On Loving God," p. 118.
17. Bernard, "On Loving God," p. 119.
18. Bernard, "On Loving God," p. 120.

The tradition of Christian spirituality is rich in its descriptions of problems met on the path to the highest stage, and there is no insistence that only by reaching this stage can one be a Christian, though it is expected that one reach at least the second stage.

Several hundred years later, Martin Luther was to describe Christian love in a less mystical, more Christ-centered, but equally moving manner. Faith, Luther wrote, "snatches us away from ourselves and puts us outside ourselves."[19] Again, "everyone should 'put on' his neighbor, and so conduct himself toward him as if he himself were in the other's place. A Christian man lives not in himself but in Christ and his neighbor. . . . He lives in Christ through faith, in his neighbor through love."[20]

The psychology of how such Christ-centered love can be possible is lucidly outlined in the following passage from Sir John Seely's *Ecco Homo* (1865):

> Now as the difficulty of discovering what is right arises commonly from the prevalence of self-interest in our minds, and as we commonly behave rightly to anyone for whom we feel affection or sympathy, Christ considered that he who could feel sympathy for all would behave rightly to all. But how to give to the meager and narrow hearts of men such enlargement? How to make them capable of a universal sympathy? Christ believed it possible to bind men to their kind, but on one condition — that they were first bound fast to Himself. He stood forth as the representative of men, He identified Himself with the cause and with the interests of all human beings, He was destined, as He began before long obscurely to intimate, to lay down His life for them. Few of us sympathize originally and directly with this devotion; few of us can perceive in human nature itself any merit sufficient to evoke it. But it is not so hard to love and venerate Him who felt it. So vast a passion of love, a devotion so comprehensive, has not elsewhere been in any degree approached, save by some of His imitators. And as love provokes love, many have found it possible to conceive for Christ an attachment the closeness of which no words can describe, a veneration so possessing and absorbing the man within them, that they have said: "I live no more, but Christ lives in me." Now such a feeling carries with it of necessity the feeling of love for all human beings. It matters no longer what quality

---

19. Martin Luther, "Treatise on Christian Liberty," in *Works* (Philadelphia: Muhlenberg Press, 1943), vol. 2, p. 342.

20. Luther, "Treatise on Christian Liberty," p. 342.

men may exhibit; amiable or unamiable, as the brothers of Christ, as belonging to His sacred and consecrated kind, as objects of His love in life and death, they must be dear to all to whom He is dear.[21]

In each case, the love of God and Christ is said to increase a person's love of others and of all creation. The Christian form of love is not an abstract caring for humanity in general, of the sort that is often found in people who have little love for anyone in particular; nor is it a love for the common aspects of all humanity found in each person. It is a strong, overflowing love of each particular human being, warts and all. However poorly most Christians live up to this goal, it is abundantly clear that Christian love has a rich and articulate theory which has inspired and changed the lives of millions, and any serious psychological theory of love must take it into account.

The defender of selfism may retort that the highest and purest form of love advocated by such humanists as Fromm has nothing to do with selfishness in any of its expressions. There are, indeed, very positive-sounding descriptions of this kind of love in Fromm's writings. For instance, he states quite explicitly that humanist self-love is the opposite of selfishness and narcissism. He defines humanist self-love as union with the loved one while preserving one's own integrity; this love involves active concern and care for the other.[22] In spite of this admittedly inspiring notion of love, the spread of self-theory psychology has resulted in a rapid dilution of the higher aspects of selfism and in more and more of the kinds of abuses we have described previously. The frequent collapse of higher selfist ideals may be attributed directly to many of the other, more fundamental concepts found in the selfist position. Fromm's nice claims about love are simply incompatible with his other, more basic psychological principles, which put all power in an autonomous self. In general, selfist theory emphasizes the isolated conscious self as the sole judge of what the self should value and how it should act. Such an emphasis guarantees the breakdown of the higher ideals into a rationalization of selfishness permeated with narcissism. Hostility toward tradition and any other authority tends to have similar effects.

Individual Christians, at least if they are serious, have many guides to

---

21. Sir John Seely, *Ecco Homo*, chap. 14; quoted in *A Diary of Readings*, comp. John Baille (New York: Scribners, 1955), Day 140.
22. Fromm, *The Art of Loving*, p. 60.

keep them away from extreme selfishness. First, there is the love of God, expressed in faith and in contemplative and meditative prayer. There is also the awareness of humanity's deep potential for sin and the need to be alert to the traps and delusions of the world. Further, there is the religious community — Christian friends, prayer groups, retreats, and the supportive aid of the church and clergy. There is the emphasis on penance, on confession (especially in prayer), Christian doctrine, the creeds, and the communion of saints. All these combine to help the practicing Christian not only to keep from surrendering to the persistent desire to return to selfism but also to arrive at higher levels of love and spiritual knowledge.

CREATIVITY AND THE CREATOR

For the selfist, creativity is conceived as personal growth through self-expression, and hence as an achievement. It is the way the individual self gains value, very often in comparison to others. In a sense, wealth, intelligence, and integrity all take a back seat today to this truly middle-class value of "creativity." Most application forms for graduate and professional schools give prominence to it, and to be labeled creative has become the ultimate goal for millions.

For Christians the emphasis is very different. It is on developing one's abilities in the service of God and others, as shown in Christ's parable of the talents. C. S. Lewis describes the Christian's indifference or antipathy to preoccupation with creativity as follows:

> Nothing could be more foreign to the tone of scripture than the language of those who describe a saint as a "moral genius" or a "spiritual genius," thus insinuating that his virtue or spirituality is "creative" or "original." If I have read the New Testament aright, it leaves no room for "creativeness" even in a modified or metaphorical sense. Our whole destiny seems to lie in the opposite direction, . . . in acquiring a fragrance that is not our own but borrowed, in becoming clean mirrors filled with the image of a face that is not ours.[23]

Therefore a Christian artist or writer should never strive for creativity per se but instead should try to embody some reflection of eternal beauty

23. C. S. Lewis, "Christianity and Literature," in *Christian Reflections,* ed. Walter Hooper (Grand Rapids: Eerdmans, 1967), pp. 6-7.

and wisdom. Lewis notes that the Christian approach to literature, for example, groups itself with certain existing theories of literature as against others. The Christian position

> would have affinities with the primitive or Homeric theory in which the poet is the mere pensioner of the Muse. It would have affinities with the Platonic doctrine of transcendent Form partly imitable on earth. . . . It would be opposed to the theory of genius as, perhaps, generally understood; and above all it would be opposed to the idea that literature is self-expression.[24]

THE NATURE OF SUFFERING

A final profound conflict between Christianity and selfism centers around the meaning of suffering. The Christian acknowledges evil — with its consequent pain, and ultimately death — as a fact of life. Through the Christian's losing his or her ordinary self in discipleship, in the imitation of Christ, such suffering can serve as the experience out of which a higher spiritual life is attained. This fundamental view is at the very heart of Christianity, as represented by the passion of the cross followed by the joy of Easter. All the great religions accept the existence of sin, illusion, and death and then provide a way to transform and transcend them. This way is always terribly difficult, but when successfully traveled it is described in the highest terms. Most of us fear the sacrifice and challenge that the true religious life presents; as a result, all over the world the genuine saint or holy person is a hero.

In contrast, selfist philosophy trivializes life by claiming that suffering (and, by implication, even death) is without intrinsic meaning. Suffering is seen as some sort of absurdity, usually a man-made mistake that could have been avoided by the use of knowledge to gain control of the environment. The selfist position sounds optimistic and plausible, particularly when advocated during materially prosperous times. But this is a superficial view, which becomes less and less convincing the more one sees of life. Millions who enthusiastically endorsed optimistic selfism in the prime of life are now beginning to experience the ancient lessons of physical decline, loss, sickness, and death — lessons that puncture all

24. Lewis, "Christianity and Literature," p. 7.

superficial optimism about the continued happy growth of the wonderful self.

What does one tell a chronically overambitious man who learns at age forty that further advancement is over and that he has a serious, possibly fatal, illness? What does one tell a woman whose early career hopes have ended in a wearisome and dead-end bureaucratic job? What does one say to the older worker who has lost his job, whose skills are not wanted? What does one tell the woman who is desperately alone inside an aging body and with a history of failed relationships? Does one advise such people to become more autonomous and independent? Does one say, "Go actualize yourself in creative activity"? For people in those circumstances, such advice is not just irrelevant, it is an insult.

It is exactly such suffering, however, that is at the center of the meaning and hope of the religious life. By starting with an unsentimental realism about existence, religion is able to provide an honest and ultimately optimistic understanding of the human condition. Christianity starts with suffering and ends with joy. Selfist-humanism starts with optimism but ends in pessimism. And its pessimism is doubly depressing, for in spite of its many religious characteristics, the selfist position is in the final analysis a kind of false or substitute religion based on denying any meaning in suffering and death, experiences from which it cannot protect us.

*   *   *

We may now summarize the critical points raised against selfism in the preceding chapters. The basic assumption of humanistic selfism — namely, the complete goodness of human nature (as opposed to the evil influence from society) — receives extremely strong criticism from a wide variety of scientists and support from remarkably few. The humanists' central concept of the conscious self is poorly defined, filled with contradictions, and seriously inadequate both as a description of our psychological nature and as a tool for serious psychotherapy. Self-theory psychology has not shown the systematic development of a traditional science, in which replicated findings and increasingly precise concepts lead one generation to build on the work of the other. Instead, self-theories have turned into popular and commercialized ideologies with concepts that are even more vague and diffuse than those of forty years ago.

The popularization of selfism is attributable in large part to the recent period of rapid economic growth in an already wealthy and secularized society, with a large and growing population of young people. Certainly it is difficult to imagine self-actualization as a popular concept except in a period of wealth and leisure. The suitability of selfism for rationalizing a consumer mentality and for justifying natural tendencies to narcissistic self-indulgence has further increased its popularity. Self-theory has been used to justify moral relativism, to facilitate divorce, and generally to undermine social cohesion and the common good. In its recent expression, the same self-theory logic has supported a widely popular but narcissistic New Age spirituality. In spite of the nonscientific character of humanistic selfism, it has frequently claimed to be or allowed itself to be taken as a science, and as a result of this misrepresentation it has gained greatly in money, power, and prestige.

Historically selfism derives from an explicitly anti-Christian humanism, and its hostility to Christianity is a logical expression of its very different assumptions about the nature of the self, of creativity, of the family, of love, and of suffering.

In short, humanistic selfism is not a science but a popular secular substitute religion, which has nourished and spread today's widespread cult of self-worship.

11. A Political Response

THE PROBLEM FOR PSYCHOLOGY

Whether or not it understands the situation, the profession of psychology finds itself in a seriously compromised position because of its advocacy of the humanist-selfist religion. An organizational symptom of this is the large Humanistic Psychology Division of the American Psychological Association (APA). The problem raised by the nonscientific character of humanistic psychology began causing serious controversy within the discipline some decades ago. Traditional psychological scientists became deeply concerned by what they saw as the erosion of the legitimate standards of objectivity for any science. D. O. Hebb very effectively expressed this concern in his 1973 presidential address to the APA. He presented the claim that psychology is a biological science and that trying to make it humanistic results in something that is neither satisfactory science nor satisfactory humanism.[1] One honest option, urged by Hebb, was for psychology to purge itself of or to shake off its religious elements and return to its original, more limited, but legitimate scientific character.

In a sense, this is what has happened in recent years. The American Psychological Association has suffered a schism. A large proportion of the research and academic psychologists have left and founded their own organization: the American Psychological Society. They gave up on the APA because of its lack of commitment to science and to objective research.[2] Meanwhile the APA has increasingly shown itself to be both

1. D. O. Hebb, "What Psychology Is About," *American Psychologist* 29 (1974): 71-79.
2. The American Psychological Society (APS) was founded in 1988 and currently

a professional society and a political/ideological interest group. It has taken stands that are quite consistent with its secular and humanistic psychology in favoring abortion and homosexual rights. Thus the APA has supported the removal of homosexuality from any official list of pathologies. A strong group of pro-homosexual activists is now pushing the APA to make even psychological treatment of homosexuals who ask to be cured of their sexual orientation a violation of professional ethics.[3] Whether this extreme expression of ideological bias will be accepted remains to be seen, but in any case the APA has become just another political interest group, lobbying for favors in Washington and elsewhere. It now has the objectivity and professional integrity of organizations such as the American Tobacco Institute.

The psychological profession's response to criticisms of its objectivity is typically to stonewall the critique, to claim that the critics are representative of idiosyncratic and isolated positions, and sometimes to attempt to redefine the notion of science or objectivity so as to conform to their own positions. This latter response ends up making the concepts of science and objectivity vague beyond any usefulness. More importantly, it also allows the traditional religions to fall clearly within the definition of science! However, humanist psychologists have no desire to allow Christian, Jewish, or other religious doctrines to intrude into "their" psychology. They just want to broaden the concept of science enough to allow their work to be categorized under such a socially, politically, and economically powerful rubric, but they do not want to allow traditional religions the advantages of the same ploy. It is exactly this intellectual misrepresentation that they have used so effectively in the advocacy of their secular faith.

Many secular and humanist psychologists seem quite willing to accept pluralism when it comes to feminist psychology or gay/lesbian psychology or black psychology, but they are unwilling to accept the same logic when it comes to Christian psychology. But the logic of

has about 15,000 members. For more information, contact their headquarters: 1010 Vermont Ave., N.W., Suite 1100, Washington, DC 20005-4907.

3. Evidence of pressure on the American Psychological Association to make treatment of homosexuality in psychotherapy a violation of APA ethical standards can be found in a statement made by Bryant L. Welch, J.D., Ph.D., on January 26, 1990, when he was Executive Director of Professional Practice for the APA. In this statement and others on APA letterhead, Welch claims that any attempt to "repair" homosexuality — even if requested by the client — is the result of heterosexual prejudice.

pluralism, once set in motion, cannot be stopped in such an arbitrary way. As a result, it seems likely that sooner or later professional psychologists will at least to some extent accept the psychology of the traditional religions as having legitimate status within an increasingly pluralistic framework. After all, if — as we noted — a Buddhist theory of personality is now acceptable in a standard textbook, why not a Christian psychology of personality? If such developments occur, much of psychology's pretension to being a science in anything like the traditional sense will be undermined. Indeed, as pluralism in psychology continues to develop, the very notion of psychology as a coherent discipline is likely to evaporate. What will actually happen in the politics of the psychological profession is hard to say, but serious, direct challenges to the status quo are certainly called for.[4]

THE PROBLEM FOR CHRISTIANITY

Although the enthusiasm for selfism has waned, an entire generation has been deeply influenced by it. Christianity, I fear, has greatly underestimated both its power and the prevalence of the institutionalization of its value system. Selfism is now the standard position of much of the government bureaucracy that deals with social problems. It is certainly the controlling system in the so-called "helping professions" — clinical psychology, counseling, and social work. Irving Kristol has aptly described the same situation as found in the education establishment:

> We have a kind of faith in the nature of people that we do not have in the botanical processes of nature itself — and I use the word "faith" in its full religious force. We really do believe that all human beings have a natural *telos* toward becoming flowers, not weeds or poison ivy, and that aggregates of human beings have a natural predisposition to arrange themselves into gardens, not jungles or garbage heaps. This sublime and noble faith we may call the religion of liberal humanism. It is the dominant spiritual and intellectual orthodoxy in America today. Indeed, despite all our chatter about the separation of church and state, one can

4. For some further discussion of this subject see P. C. Vitz, "Escaping the Secular Enlightenment but Slouching Toward Yugoslavia: A Response to Watson," *International Journal of Psychology of Religion* 3 (1993): 21-24.

even say it is the official religion of American society today, as against which all other religions can be criticized as divisive and parochial.[5]

The reason for this dominance is clear. The government bureaucracy in general, and the "helping professions" in particular, must have an ethic by which to set goals and priorities and evaluate procedures. This ethic must be noncontroversial yet also inspiring if it is to be justified to the legislature and the electorate. Programs that are "for people" and that "help you help yourself" are the most positive among the lowest common denominators available.

In frequent contacts with clinical psychologists, I have found humanism almost unanimous. When a Christian view is mentioned, they are, today, far more likely to be alarmed than they were in the 1970s when I first wrote this book; then they acted amused, as though they were being shown an antique. But in either case, if the suggestion of Christian withdrawal from or revolt against selfist values is made, the reaction is (as it was) one of anger or irritation. Psychologists today are indifferent to Christianity because they rarely hear it advocated in their professional environment; but when it is brought to their attention, the hostility is clear.

Fifty years ago the "helping professions" were of little consequence; today they are huge and still growing as the government expands its social services. The accompaniment of this growth by the self-theory ethic constitutes a powerful challenge to the Christian faith. There is little reason to believe that this secular religion will change over the years, since it is not some arbitrary choice based on a fad in the 1960s but a necessary part of the extension of government programs into every aspect of our personal and family life. This expansion of the state will continue until it either meets resistance or simply collapses of its own weight. In any event, a secular ideology is a necessity for a secular state — and as a result, it becomes harder and harder to be both a good Christian and a good American.

Let us look briefly at some of the particular policies expressing selfism through government programs. One area staked out by these secular humanists is the "science" of thanatology, or Death and Dying (D & D), as it is often called. New journals, government-sponsored re-

5. Irving Kristol, "Thoughts on Reading About a Number of Summer-Camp Cabins Covered with Garbage," *The New York Times Magazine,* 17 Nov. 1974, p. 38.

search institutes, D & D study courses, and the like have turned death into the newest intellectual growth industry. Malachi Martin has characterized the main theory of death guiding this movement as follows: "Death is transformed for everyone from a Doorway into a Wall."[6] That is, the religious concept of life after death is denied (more accurately, ignored, and death is interpreted as the absolute end. The essentially religious nature of this problem is clear, and we see again government-sponsored programs and philosophy challenging and competing with Christianity.

The most striking example today is the realm of sex education programs in secondary and even in primary schools — now, as early as the first grade. The country is filled with high schools where the principal pushes condoms while militantly rejecting any reference even to the name of God. And of course reading, writing, and arithmetic have long since been left on the back burner of the educational system, in favor of what is now commonly called "affective education" (e.g., self-esteem).

The initial ideological orientation of the sex education programs was to exclude consideration of all aspects of sex except its biological aspects, plus a few social consequences. But this denial of the moral, religious, and spiritual character of sexual relations is a biased control of the ground rules for understanding sex. This bias guarantees an antireligious presentation of sex to students, as well as facilitating an aggressive desacralization of sexual love. Thus the secular value system is expanded. In terms of a legal analogy, the meaning and purpose of sex are on trial in the classroom, and the religious defense is not allowed to speak or even to be present. This denial of due process for the religious view within secular education is justified on the ground that a biological presentation is scientific and totally objective.

Complaints about the exclusion of the religious interpretation of sex cannot be dismissed as merely the expected position of a bunch of sexually repressed, moralistic, modern-day Puritans; instead, it is to be found among the most sensitive and sophisticated psychological thinkers. We quote again from Ernest Becker, who presents his own views as well as the psychoanalyst Otto Rank's understanding of this problem:

The questions about sex that the child asks are thus not — at a fundamental level — about sex at all. They are about the meaning of the body,

6. Malachi B. Martin, "Death at Sunset," *National Review*, 22 Nov. 1974, p. 1356.

the terror of living with a body. When the parents give a straightforward biological answer to sexual questions, they do not answer the child's question at all. He wants to know why he has a body, where it came from, and what it means for a self-conscious creature to be limited by it. He is asking about the ultimate mystery of life, not about the mechanics of sex. As Rank says, this explains why the adults suffer as much from the sexual problem as the child: the "biological solution of the problem of humanity is ungratifying and inadequate for the adult as for the child."

Sex is a "disappointing answer to life's riddle," and if we pretend that it is an adequate one, we are lying both to ourselves and to our children. As Rank beautifully argues, in this sense "sex education" is a kind of wishful thinking, a rationalization, and a pretense: we try to make believe that if we give instruction in the mechanics of sex we are explaining the mystery of life. We might say that modern man tries to replace vital awe and wonder with a "How to do it" manual. We know why: if you cloak the mystery of creation in the easy steps of human manipulations you banish the terror of the death that is reserved for us as species-sexual animals. Rank goes so far as to conclude that the child is sensitive to this kind of lying. He refuses the "correct scientific explanation" of sexuality, and he refuses too the mandate to guilt-free sex enjoyment that it implies.[7]

A detailed documentation of how tax money is used to support the cult of self-worship is beyond the scope of this book, but certainly the major way this happens is through the massive tax support of education and, through education, many other activities of the "helping professions." From Stanford and Harvard down to the local elementary school, the education of most Americans is permeated with selfist ideology. Prominent graduate schools turn out articulate proponents of these values, who readily find responsible positions in bureaucracies, big business, and the media, where their newly acquired selfist religion continues to feed the secularization process. There should be no illusions about the attitudes that are prevalent in these institutions: Christianity is dismissed as a foolish, uncultured, bigoted remnant of premodern superstition. Pluralism is advocated as a disguise for secular humanist control of religions through the government/university/big business apparatus.

7. Ernest Becker, *The Denial of Death* (New York: Free Press/Macmillan, 1973), p. 164.

Religion is seen as, at best, a form of local color that is sometimes interesting, at worst as a fundamentalist attack on their never-questioned secular "verities"; it is never personally convincing to those who believe that their consciousness has been raised above such limited earlier forms of thought.

These people exclude religion, and delete even the name of God from our textbooks,[8] and then complain that when parents want these put back *in* it is the parents who are guilty of censorship! This dishonest position is commonly espoused by many liberals, who claim to represent the American way.

That Christians are taxed to support large-scale programs that regularly teach anti-Christian theories is not just a serious case of intellectual misrepresentation; it has become a grave violation of the constitutional separation of church and state. Violation of this separation in the past typically has come from undue religious involvement in secular functions. It should come as no surprise that with the massive growth of government the situation is now reversed: the secular system, which intrudes into all aspects of life, has been using government-funded and government-controlled programs for propagating its own faith.

Conservative Christians too often intuitively recognize the nature of these conflicts without being able to articulate their position with much sophistication. Meanwhile, the liberal churches have often enthusiastically embraced selfism and humanistic psychology without regard to their hostility to Christian teaching. It seems high time to transcend both reactions with a postmodern, intellectually sound counterresponse. Healthy signs of such a reaction are the growth of the home school movement and the founding of many new Christian schools. In any event, we must regain for the church the large, legitimate religious issues that it has surrendered to secular ideologies like selfist psychology.

In addition to the development of an intellectual critique of secularism, a Christian political response is called for. I do not mean by this "politics as usual" — in the sense of ideological conflicts between left and right — for the usual ideologies of both capitalism and Communism are essentially secular, and in their modern forms both are anti-Christian. Nor am I suggesting rallies, demonstrations, or new political parties. What seems more to the point is the quiet but persistent long-term

8. See, e.g., Paul C. Vitz, *Censorship: Evidence of Bias in Our Children's Textbooks* (Ann Arbor: Servant Publications, 1986).

withdrawal of support from the anti-Christian activities of the modern state, whether these emerge from the "left" (e.g., the public school system), the "right" (e.g., the Central Intelligence Agency), or the "middle of the road" (e.g., the Internal Revenue Service).

The exact form that this defense of the faith might take depends on particular circumstances. It does not fall within my intention here to develop a theory of Christian political action in response to government-sponsored hostility to Christianity. But more legal challenges by Christians to tax-supported secularization are called for. Public education — which is in effect *government* education, selfist in orientation and hostile to religion — is certainly one area of importance here, since unfortunately, in many parts of the country, the public schools have become a public menace. Therefore, serious consideration has to be given to the implications of keeping one's children in public schools; enrolling them in existing Christian schools or establishing new schools will often be a preferable course of action. In many cases, support can be withdrawn from government schools by voting against taxes, or by encouraging vouchers and other forms of choice that give some kind of financial fair treatment to religious schools. It is worth noting here that the people most in favor of vouchers are commonly the inner-city poor. These are the parents and children most victimized by the incompetent secular educational bureaucracies.

Christian college alumni should reflect on the directions currently being taken by the colleges they attended, rather than automatically responding to the annual pleas for financial contributions on the strength of fond memories of an older atmosphere, long since superseded. Why donate money where your gift will be used to undermine the faith of young people? Investigate ways of giving money that will help support your religion rather than another selfist professor. Scholarship funds for Christian students may be an example of this. If a son or daughter is thinking of going to a secular school, ask the administration (not the local churches) what sort of environment is provided for the encouragement and development of students' spiritual lives. How does that environment compare with the environments provided to encourage and develop students' athletic, social, and sex lives — that is, to advance secularism?

A persistent Christian withdrawal from government-controlled schooling, combined with the continued growth of Christian education, could have profound effects. The secular establishment, however indifferent to or contemptuous of religion, does depend on broad public support. Withdrawal of such support, along with the development of alternative educational systems by Christians, could greatly reduce the size and influence of the present secular system. Such a goal is not unreasonable, since the public schools are already extremely costly, terribly inefficient, and suffering from a well-deserved and growing loss of public trust, as well as a growing lack of self-confidence. Furthermore, as America's population continues to age, the pressure to move limited tax monies from education to medical costs can only grow.

Secular education has drained so much of the higher meaning out of higher education that students everywhere now see getting an education almost exclusively in terms of finding a job. Religious, spiritual, moral, and ethical ideals have all but disappeared, and with this disappearance, wisdom and knowledge have degenerated into mere information, usually of a kind that rapidly becomes obsolete. No wonder parents and students are becoming more and more skeptical about "higher education," especially at a cost of many thousands of dollars a year. But it is exactly this higher meaning, which is necessary for any education to be of intrinsic importance, that religion can supply.

12. Beyond the Secular Self

THE BIAS IN BEING "OBJECTIVE"

The assumption that the objective method of science is a fair and un-biased procedure for correctly understanding a phenomenon is widely accepted in modern society. I shall argue here, as a final major criticism of selfism, that, used in the study of human beings, this method is a profoundly prejudiced ideological tool, which leads inevitably to a par-ticular theory of humankind. Furthermore, the objective method is in-timately connected with the growth of the modern self; specifically, it is proposed that the procedure of being objective is the fundamental psychological operation behind the growth of the self.

Before the case for the preceding claim is developed, it is necessary briefly to discuss the paradoxical relation of humanistic selfism to the objective method of science. A central argument of Rogers, May, and others is that the objective method is seriously inadequate for under-standing human beings. The existentialists also asserted that psychol-ogy is intrinsically incapable of being a satisfactory natural science. Now, in psychotherapy the objective method requires that the therapist interpret the patient through evidence such as scores on personality tests, and as exemplifying a category in some theory. That is, the therapist responds to the patient in terms of analytical and reasoning capacities. The selfists reject this as seriously inadequate, and in con-trast place great emphasis on the therapist's ability to identify with the patient, to empathize uncritically with him or her. This humanist critique of the objective method represents a major argument about the limitations of science. In this respect, it is not only consistent with but also very supportive of a religious interpretation of human nature,

Christian or otherwise; here religion is clearly indebted to the humanists.

Unfortunately, in spite of the selfists' theoretical arguments about the psychotherapeutic relationship, for millions of people who have read and been influenced by them the actual consequences have been exactly the opposite. Self-theory has turned each person's self as it is experienced by him or her into more of an object than ever before. Never have so many people been so self-conscious, so aware of the self as something to be expressed, defended, and so forth. The self has become an object to itself. People talk about their self-image, their self-actualization, or their self-esteem in the same way they used to talk about their social status, their car, or their stomach ulcers.

There is another unfavorable consequence of the selfist position. The emphasis on empathy and identification with others (for instance, the touching and feeling encouraged in encounter groups) has led to an overreaction against reason and objectivity. One result has been a cultivation of the irrational in therapy, the rejection of reason, and a lowering of perfectly legitimate standards for training psychotherapists.[1] From the Christian and Jewish points of view, neither uncontrolled, mindless intuition nor too rigidly controlled, emotionless reason is acceptable. With these points made, we can begin the final critique of selfism.

Objectification is an intellectual act, central to all criticism, which takes a naive, unexamined experience and turns the source or cause of the experience into an object of study. That is, to *objectify*, as the word implies, is to take an unself-conscious experience, in which the self and external cause are fused, and break it into a subject and object. The self is the subject, and the object is the outside cause of the *e*xperience. This action creates a "distance" between subject (self) and object, which allows the object to be examined. The spatial analogy of distance is not defined precisely, but the point is that unself-conscious experience ("fusion") is like physical commingling of self and object, and objectification, or self-conscious knowledge, is like the self's stepping away from the object, hence creating a distance and an "angle" of observation for the critical self.

The earliest or first state is the natural state of naiveté, which char-

---

1. See Hans H. Strupp, "Clinical Psychology, Irrationalism, and the Erosion of Excellence," *American Psychologist* 21 (1976): 561-71; and Paul Meehl, *Psychodiagnosis* (Minneapolis: University of Minnesota Press, 1973).

acterizes much of childhood and presumably the early historical periods of a society. The self-theorists' emphasis on empathy as a source of interpersonal knowledge represents a preoccupation on their part with a technique that to a limited extent recaptures the mentality of this first state. The second state is a period of increasing critical distancing — of denial of innocence — which gathers momentum as one new object after another is brought under study. The history of ideas is in many respects the history of the discovery of previously unexamined experiences, which then serve as new objects of study.

The process of objectifying experience is fundamentally the process of treating events as though they were objects. Early in life, when the child distinguishes between his or her own body and things external to it, objectification works well. In fact, psychologists describe this process as individuation, that is, the successive separation from outside "objects" (most objects being people). But when human beings are treated more and more objectively, various problems arise. The development of objective knowledge intrinsically involves a power relationship: the subject (self) has power over the object. In psychology, for instance, the development of objective knowledge about people requires experiments in which the experimenter has increasingly greater control (another name for power) over the person studied. The development of science is largely determined by the rate at which new techniques provide more precise control over the objects studied. To be treated as an object is to be under the power of the subject (self) who is studying you.

> The very terminology, *subject* and *object*, has an independent power quotient in grammar, where *subject* connotes activity and *object* passivity (note the verbal form *to subject!*), with the suggestion of the division of reality between animate and inanimate, agents and things, beholder and beheld.[2]

Since objective knowledge is based on the subject's controlling power over the object, it follows that any distinction between subject and object is inevitably a power distinction and therefore also a moral distinction. This well-known relationship is often expressed in the complaint "You're treating me like an object." Women quite rightly complain when they

2. Walter Wink, *The Bible in Human Transformation* (Philadelphia: Fortress, 1973), pp. 25-26.

are treated as sex objects, but the answer to this is surely not a mutual, competitive power struggle in which both women and men get treated as objects. Yet this is exactly what the scientifically "objective" approach encourages — while claiming to be an unbiased, morally neutral procedure for discovering truth.

It is this underlying bias that explains the ideological conflict over sex education. The entire biological presentation in sex education is a treatment of men, women, and sex as objects. The problem is not just that the religious view of sexual relations is excluded; it is that the morally loaded "objective" view dominates: people and sex become objects. The ultimate ploy of the advocates of sex education programs is to keep people from becoming aware of this bias by talking about the "objective scientific" nature of the biology of sex. Even when the opponents firmly sense the existence of bias, they often founder when it comes to conscious articulation of it.

THE OBJECT'S REVENGE

The power gained by the self as it objectifies more and more objects that come under its increasingly sophisticated control feeds self-growth or individuation. The process is experienced as actualization, as becoming autonomous, becoming independent of the objects — the places, people, and customs — now located "outside," in the environment with which the self was first unself-consciously fused.

One outcome of this objective view so common today is well described by Hans Jonas:

> Modern theory is about objects lower than man: even stars, being common things, are lower than man. . . . [Even in human sciences, whose object *is* man,] their object too is "lower than man". . . . For a scientific theory of him to be possible, man, including his habits of valuation, has to be taken as determined by causal laws, as an instance and part of nature. The scientist does take him so — but not himself while he assumes and exercises his freedom of inquiry and his openness to reason, evidence, and truth. Thus man-the-knower apprehends man-*qua*-lower-than-himself and in doing so achieves knowledge of man-*qua*-lower-than-man, since all scientific theory is of things lower than man-the-knower. It is on that condition that they can be subject to "theory," hence to control, hence to use. Then man-lower-than-man explained

by the human sciences — man reified — can by the instructions of these sciences be controlled (even "engineered") and thus used.[3]

Clearly, the price of this growth is considerable, and in time it becomes intolerable. If the subject is master and the object is slave, then in true Hegelian fashion there ultimately occurs what can only be described as the "object's revenge." The object eventually conquers by reducing the subject to the object's categorical level. Again, as Jonas puts it:

> And as the use of what is lower-than-man can only be for what is lower and not for what is higher in the user himself, the knower and user becomes in such use, if made all-inclusive, himself lower than man. . . . Inevitably the manipulator comes to see himself in the same light as those his theory has made manipulable; and in the self-inclusive solidarity with the general human lowliness amidst the splendor of human power his charity is but self-compassion and that tolerance that springs from self-contempt: we are all poor puppets and cannot help being what we are.[4]

The master becomes defined by his slaves, the subject by its objects, the psychologist by his rats or pigeons or cats.[5]

THE DILEMMA OF EXISTENTIAL NARCISSISM

Another and simultaneous revenge is a result of the terrible distance and consequent alienation from the objectified others. Naturally enough, this distance creates an intense need for closeness, for love. When the distanced and controlled object is an automobile or a computer, few problems result. When the process distances the self from spouse, parents, brothers and sisters, lovers — finally from almost everyone — the situation becomes desperate.

---

3. Hans Jonas, *The Phenomenon of Life* (New York: Harper & Row, 1966), pp. 195-96; quoted in Wink, *The Bible in Human Transformation*, pp. 39-40.

4. Jonas, *The Phenomenon of Life*, p. 196; quoted in Wink, *The Bible in Human Transformation*, p. 40.

5. Just to teach psychology or to run experiments is to participate in the morality of the subject-object distinction. Indeed, perhaps the appeal of "objective" psychological theories is that they give power to the selves of those who understand and use them. This power is certainly the primary appeal of the popular "you-can-win-at-the-game-of-life" books discussed earlier.

Some of the frightening, even pathetic responses to this developing situation have been poignantly described by Herbert Hendin in *The Age of Sensation,* a psychoanalytic exploration of several hundred college-age young people. The students described were from Columbia and Barnard Colleges and are not necessarily typical of the country, but they are representative of intelligent, upper-middle-class college youth from the country's major urban and suburban centers. Throughout the book there is not a single mention of religion as playing a part in the life of any of the students. As far as one can gather, the students and their families are living entirely without religious values. In this the students are characteristic of a generation reared almost entirely on humanist values and self-psychology.

Hendin starts by defining this generation in terms of "its active pursuit of disengagement, detachment, fragmentation, and emotional numbness."

> The students I saw tried many escape routes. The main ones moved in two seemingly different directions: one toward numbness and limited, controlled experience; the other toward impulsive action and fragmented sensory stimulation. At times the same student alternated between one and the other. To perform, but not to feel, to acquire sensory experiences without emotional involvement were hopes which reflect the consuming wish not to know or acknowledge one's feelings.[6]

He goes on to describe their thoroughly selfist motives:

> This culture is marked by a self-interest and egocentrism that increasingly reduce all relations to the question: What am I getting out of it?
> . . . Society's fascination with self-aggrandizement makes many young people judge all relationships in terms of winning and losing points.
>
> For both sexes in this society, caring deeply for anyone is becoming synonymous with losing. Men seem to want to give women less and less, while women increasingly see demands men make as inherently demeaning.[7]

In such an emotional climate, romantic and idealistic heterosexual love relationships are rare. Part of the distancing between the sexes can be seen in the increase in homosexual relationships.[8]

---

6. Herbert Hendin, *The Age of Sensation* (New York: Norton, 1975), p. 6.
7. Hendin, *The Age of Sensation,* p. 13.
8. Contemporary homosexual activism has been a major contributor to the tendency

Hendin's description of the family life of one of these young women fits easily into a selfist model:

> She described her parents as "nice, pleasure-loving people" who are "sort of like camp counselors." She added that she "sort of liked" some of her counselors, even though she was miserable at camp. She said, "My parents aren't the sort who feel the family has to do something on a Sunday, so if they are together they get along fine because they are doing things that independently they want to do. If it happens that two of them want to do something at the same time, then it's OK. If they all had to go to the zoo together, they'd probably kill each other. They're better than families who feel they have to be together. My parents aren't the type who sacrifice themselves for their children. I don't think parents should."[9]

These highly selfist families are so captured by cultural values that they no longer provide a haven from the outside world. Instead, the family is a center of self-aggrandizement, exploitativeness, and titillation.

Hendin often provides a clinical critique of selfism, one related to that presented here earlier:

> People out of touch with their feelings are strongly drawn to the idea that life consists of playing roles. Game playing (transactional analysis) goes even further in providing a model for how to deal with other people without even considering one's feelings toward them; . . . game playing is a parody of our concern with mastery and control.[10]

As a consequence of this emphasis,

> Society is fomenting depression in the trend toward the devaluation of children and the family. The increasing emphasis on solitary gratification and immediate, tangible gain from all relationships only encourages an unwillingness in parents to give of themselves or tolerate the demands of small children.[11]

---

to treat men as sex objects. For example, the various rapidly growing male homosexual magazines commonly feature men as sex objects for other men; magazines such as *Playgirl* (a reverse mimic of *Playboy*), which are ostensibly for women, are reported to have a heavy homosexual readership.

9. Hendin, *The Age of Sensation,* p. 296.

10. Hendin, *The Age of Sensation,* p. 332.

11. Hendin, *The Age of Sensation,* pp. 257-58.

Hendin's descriptions portray exactly where so much of selfism ends: the self as subject frantically trying to gain control over others — the objects — in order to build its own self as subject. As more and more people have their "consciousness raised" — that is, as they are "liberated" from objecthood and take on the role of subjects — the competition becomes fierce. Life has become a game where there are only two states: winning and losing; sadist and masochist. Furthermore, the new role of subject carries with it the almost unbearable memory of having been an exploited object in the past. This, plus the threat that the same thing might possibly happen in the future, raises to a high pitch the need to be the dominant subject. Intimate personal relationships become extremely dangerous. If you show weakness, such as a need for love, you get slaughtered; if you withdraw to a machine-like, emotion-free competence and develop complete identification with career, you are isolated and starved for intimacy and love. Perhaps there is some relief in temporarily losing the self in sexual or other sensations and afterwards counting each new experience as a score for the self, but a lonely, deathlike living is inescapable.

This painful double bind leaves love of the self as the diabolically "safe" alternative. The trap cannot be avoided because it follows the fundamental logic of self-actualization, with its aim of developing the existential, autonomous self. Therefore this syndrome might be called "existential narcissism." There are other kinds of narcissism that result from neurotic experiences such as an unstable or overindulgent childhood, but existential narcissism follows from a modern approach to living often chosen in adult life. Its end is the psychological death (in some cases, the physical death as well) of the self. Death may come from greater and greater devotion to sensation (sex, violence, or drugs) or from retreat into the isolated, machine-like world of the careerist ego — cold, calculating, often fueled by amphetamines. In either case there is an ever-tightening, self-inflicted solitary confinement based on continually repressing the need for love.

ESCAPE FROM THE SELF

Stage 1: The Naive Self or the Self as Object

As stated above, at first the self and object are fused in the naive unselfconscious experience commonly found in children. This stage generally ends because the principle of objectification is intrinsic to human beings and develops naturally with maturity as one compares and reflects on wider and wider domains of experience. The very young child first learns to distinguish the physical boundaries between self and the objects and people in his or her surrounding world. The Rogerian and Frommian emphases on empathy and identification with the client or loved one are conscious strategies for recapturing the Stage 1 kind of knowledge. This is a legitimate, but limited, technique. Its great danger is that it easily degenerates into the search for sensations, such as drugs, sex, or violence, as part of a general overreaction against reason.

Stage 2: The Selfist Self or the Self as Subject

The process of distinguishing the self from other entities — called objectification — develops as a person expands into new types of experience, until social customs, the values, beliefs, and personality characteristics of others, and finally the self are objectified. This activity of turning more and more experience into objectified knowledge creates power derived from the objects that the self controls. Using this power, the selfist self, or the self as subject, continues to grow and expand. The willing decision continually to increase this power can be called the Faustian bargain — a "bondage of the will" at the center of contemporary hubris. The price of this "bargain" is the large-scale alienation from objectified others and the loneliness seen in much of modern literature and film — a loneliness common throughout our society. Objective science is, of course, the major conscious cultural expression of this mode of thought.

Stage 2 finally ends when even the self and the very principle of objectification are seen as objects. Once this happens, suspicion of the self as subject and suspicion of the process of being objective have begun. The quest for the authentic self is now seen as inauthentic. This suspicion is starting to spread throughout the West. It is manifest, however imperfectly, in the growing suspicion of science, technology, business, and government (i.e., suspicion of objectification and the systems based on it). It is also manifest in suspicion of the self, exemplified in the wide appeal of New Age spirituality, with its drugs and mystical experience, in which loss of the modern self occurs.

These symptoms of the suspicion of a mentality that has been basic to the West since the Renaissance are too varied and too natural an extension of modern thought to be dismissed as temporary aberrations. They signal that the waning of the modern age has begun.

Stage 3: The Transcendent Self or the Self as God's Object

The resolution of the preceding dilemma is religious, not psychological, and I shall describe it here in Christian terms. Very simply, the only way out is to lose the self, to let it go, and once more willingly to become an object again — not an object naively fused with the flow of life (since except for brief moments this is no longer possible), nor an object to be controlled by other selves acting as subjects, but an object in the love and the service of God.

In order for this to happen, one must let go of the selfist self and of its controlling will, bloated from constructing the interior apparatus of secular competence. This letting go is no easy task, yet it is an essential one. With preparation of mind and will, transcendent awareness of God's love and will is possible by God's grace.

The movement to Stage 3 is never perfect or complete. It can occur in many ways. For some the change is sudden and intensely emotional — a conversion like that of St. Paul. For others it is the struggling development and maintenance of the true mystical life as represented by St. Bernard or St. Theresa. For still others it is the slow, often sporadic development of a sense of being guided by divine Providence. In all of these cases, reason plays a major role, indeed a necessary one, for feelings become distorted or vague or grow cold. In all of these cases, prayer is essential. However short or long the period of transformation, it is aptly called a second birth.

The conditions that remove barriers and facilitate the movement to this stage provide a field of study for a Christian spiritual psychology (a field hardly in existence in any modern form). Although knowledge may be helpful in preparing for the transcendent stage, the major barrier is not lack of knowledge but the presence of the self's will to power. It is precisely for this reason that the New Testament is so thoroughly characterized by motives and metaphors that are directly antithetical to the psychology of the independent, rebellious, autonomous, self-created self.

> Truly, I say to you, unless you turn and become like children, you will never enter the kingdom of heaven. Whoever humbles himself like this child, he is greatest in the kingdom of heaven. (Matt. 18:3-4)

The same concern is expressed over and over — for example, when Christians are called the servants of God, and when the Lord is called our shepherd.

The third stage has important similarities to the first. It can be interpreted in part, in the familiar phrase of Paul Ricoeur, as a "second naïveté."[12]

There is little doubt that Stage 3 can be painfully difficult to reach. And pulpits filled with talk about autonomous, self-actualized, self-determined, self-conscious, independently creative, OK selves don't make the process any easier.

In conclusion, some personal remarks. The hardest ideas to deal with are those of the type just described, ideas that "threaten my ego." In spite of my rejection of self-theory, large parts of me remain that are still thoroughly indoctrinated with it. Particularly difficult are religious ideas such as penitence, humility, accepting my dependence on God, and praying for help. In my heart and in my mind I know that these are good, true, and necessary for spiritual life. I know that they are needed to curb pride and to purge arrogance. But my yet luxuriant, overblown ego balks at and rejects being labeled "a miserable offender," wonders about the need for repentance, and occasionally bristles at metaphors referring to me as a sheep, child, or obedient servant. Equally foreign is the concept of judgment.

I know that many others who are not as ready as I am to listen are turned away by these words at once. The justification for these concepts has been lost, and reeducation is desperately needed. We need updated

12. Paul Ricoeur, *Symbolism of Evil* (New York: Harper & Row, 1967), p. 351. Ricoeur writes: "if we can no longer live the great symbolisms of the sacred in accordance with the original belief in them, we can, we modern men, aim at a second naïveté in and through criticism." Criticism such as the present work only aims at the second naiveté; it is not the second naiveté itself. The kind of thinking characteristic of the third or transcendent stage is qualitatively different from modern criticism, which is still part of the Stage 2 mentality. True "second naiveté" thought is expressed most perfectly in Jesus Christ, less perfectly in the lives of the great spiritual leaders and saints. In a psychoanalytic framework, Stage 1 thought can be understood as primary process thinking; Stage 2 thinking is secondary process thought — the reality testing behind ego development. Taking this logic a step further, I would argue that there exists what should be called tertiary thinking, which qualitatively transcends secondary thinking.

orthodox theology. We need sermons on radical obedience, on the mysticism of submissive surrender of the will, on the beauty of dependency, on how to find humility. We all know that it is hard for a rich person to get to heaven; I'm certain that it is even harder for someone with a Ph.D. The problem for Ph.D.s — and I include here doctors, lawyers, and professionals of all kinds — is the problem of pride and will. In spite of our resistance, we all need to hear something that will improve our odds!

13. A New Christian Future?

THE END OF MODERN HEROISM

Disillusionment with modern society is familiar and widespread. The basic cause for this is the failure of secular heroic models to convince us of their intrinsic worth. We have consumed the heroic meaning in modernist life. The heroes are dead; even the anti-heroes have gone stale. (The heroines aren't doing very well either.) The Great Revolutionary has dwindled to a part in political theater. The Communist hero is now . . . Castro? The Socialist ideal is a fading bore. Traditional politics has become a media-manipulated process of image control, in which show drives out substance, leaving the viewer with a residue of minor sentiments. The sports hero is a commercialized entertainer at best, a money-grubber at worst. Today extraordinary salaries are often paid to quite mediocre players, who can in no way be perceived as "heroes." Physical adventure and exploration have long since given way to the occasional self-conscious, artificial creation of challenge, such as rowing across the Atlantic Ocean or climbing up a mountain backwards. The heroic military ideal, destroyed by the impersonal, frightening destructiveness of modern war, has degenerated into the nostalgic reenactment of old battles in which a person's courage and daring once made a difference. The idea of a scientist as hero has eroded until all that remains is the cold brilliance of a super-administrator leading a team of technicians in a bureaucratic enterprise sponsored by some government, reported at a fancy international convention, and covered by the ever-present press; or, worse still, there is the growing role of the anti-hero scientist, who confronts us with lawsuits over who discovered what first, or with faked data, or with the realities of genetic engineering or more efficient mind control.

163

The crisis is held at bay by millions of individuals attempting to find heroic meaning in the private neuroses of their personal careers. They fantasize tough-minded accomplishment surrounded by the soft rewards of various pleasures: stoical existentialism at work, epicurean consumerism at play. This double theme of a successful career combined with sensational, often decadent pleasure is standard with such women's magazines as *Cosmopolitan*. Their advertising and articles show the contemporary social value attached to the two responses of career and consumerism, the crippling strategies of so many. Multinational corporations and government bureaucracies alike need hard-working professional types who are not tied down and are interchangeable across organizations, people who promptly spend their salaries to keep the consumer economy going.

The pathetic inadequacy of hedonistic pleasure as a route to higher meaning soon becomes obvious. One generation at most can pretend that such a "quest" is "heroic"; its degrading triviality cannot be long disguised. As Becker puts it:

> Hedonism is not heroism for most men. The pagans in the ancient world did not realize that and so lost out to the "despicable" creed of Judeo-Christianity. Modern men equally do not realize it, and so they sell their souls to consumer capitalism . . . or replace their souls — as Rank said — with psychology. Psychotherapy is such a growing vogue today because people want to know why they are unhappy in hedonism and look for faults within themselves.[1]

THE FAILURE OF CAREERISM

The ideal of a career is beginning to sputter. Large numbers of the professions are now glutted, and it has become hard to think that the world needs more lawyers (even women lawyers!). In addition, the narcissistic focus needed to maintain a career orientation leads to a kind of social isolation; those who are intensely preoccupied with themselves and their personal goals commonly sacrifice marriage, family, and friends. Even if the career is successful, the social isolation regularly drains away any sense of contentment or satisfaction. By the time you reach your forties, the world of career can seem pretty bleak.

1. Ernest Becker, *The Denial of Death* (New York: Free Press/Macmillan, 1973), p. 268.

In part, career failure has resulted from the disappearance of other higher and supporting ideals. The universities, centers of selfist values, have unrealistically encouraged careerism for a pragmatic reason: they desperately need enrollments to stay in business. But the universities have also disparaged and ground down all other ideals. Faculty members pushing pluralistic relativism have destroyed once-common forms of idealism. As a result, the romance of the career — unsupported by such ideals as truth (for those in education), justice (for those in law), patriotism (for those in the military), life (for those in medicine) — soon collapses into just a job. In this respect, Bellah and his colleagues note: "The absence of a sense of calling means an absence of a sense of moral meaning."[2]

Other reasons for the collapse of careerism have included the unrealistically high expectations for success of so many young people over the past thirty years. After all, when everyone is "the most important person in the whole wide world" there is some downside risk. Moreover, economic growth in the United States has slowed considerably, and it is unlikely to come close to matching that of the post–World War II decades. Any major economic trouble in the coming years would only make matters worse. In addition, a very high proportion of today's career opportunities are in large organizations or bureaucracies. Such cumbersome systems invariably limit opportunities for advancement and destroy chances for effective, gratifying action. These large systems also lay off people quite casually and provide little sense of a work community.

Let us also note that many people have chosen careers, not because they were truly "ambitious," but because it was the thing to do. Often they had no real interest in the activity involved. The sacrifices that careers typically require are particularly meaningless to such people.[3]

Finally — and most importantly — careers are intrinsically too weak an ideal to carry the huge psychic burden that has been laid upon them.

2. Robert N. Bellah, Richard Madsen, William M. Sullivan, Ann Swidler, and Steven M. Tipton, *Habits of the Heart: Individualism and Commitment in American Life* (New York: Harper & Row, 1985), p. 71.

3. Over the last twenty-five years I have discussed psychology careers with at least two thousand different undergraduates — mostly psychology majors. In recent years, more and more of them are choosing careers for extrinsic reasons — for example, because of their parents, or because of the need for some kind of goal after college. Today it is the well-socialized student who goes on to graduate training in some career; it is the unusual, imaginative, and interesting student who does not.

As noted above, even among that small number of people who find great career success, only a few are truly satisfied; many lead lives that are sad and empty. Who, on his or her deathbed, was ever heard to say: "If only I'd spent more time at the office!"

THE TRIBALIST TEMPTATION

To a substantial degree, the concept "postmodern" really means "anti-modern"; thus it is postmodern to be anti-science, anti-reason, anti-city, anti-business, anti-state, anti-bigness — and, increasingly, anti-secular as well.

Hence, in many respects, our society has already begun to move decisively away from modern secularism and the secular self and toward some new set of ideals and heroes. Unfortunately, the new heroes seem to be increasingly tribal in nature. Racial, ethnic, and religious identities, once submerged in the modern bureaucratic society, are now being rediscovered in all their particularism. (The "melting pot" only melted identities that were quite similar to begin with.) Much of Eastern Europe is coming unglued, along ethnic and religious lines. India suffers from major internal religious conflict. Italy and Canada appear headed for some kind of breakup. Separatist and secessionist movements are surfacing around the globe. Here in America the question of what can hold us together is on the minds of most thoughtful observers of the social and political scene.

Many have been dissatisfied with our three major television networks. But at least the millions viewing them have been an American community. We will soon have several hundred channels to choose among, and the splintering potential for our society of this new range of choices is vast. Perhaps we were only held together by our fear of the Soviet Union and communism. In any case, the absence of a serious external threat to the country guarantees that internal conflicts will become increasingly severe.

In responding to the crisis of tribalism, humanistic psychology can be of no use whatsoever.[4] After all, it is based upon personal moral

---

4. Arthur Schlesinger, Jr., in *The Disuniting of America* (New York: Norton, 1992), has very effectively described today's political pluralism and its destructive implications for American social order. Contemporary pluralism contains within it the seeds of a

relativity, in which each ego is, as it were, a sovereign tribe. From self-actualization to values clarification, social anarchy is the inevitable and logical consequence of the relativity of modern secular and humanistic society. Choose your own values — follow your bliss — and forget about everybody else. Don't let anyone lay their values on you!

The universities, with their deep commitment to permissiveness and pluralism, have actively fostered this kind of intellectual and moral nihilism. Deconstructionists have powerfully argued that no written text has any fixed meaning, that all interpretation lies in the beholder; and thus we see individual moral relativism being advocated at the highest intellectual levels. Values clarification for the kids; deconstruction for graduate students. Meanwhile, feminists, gay and lesbian advocates, and other minority groups are arguing that all truth (especially morality) is ideological. At present, this intellectual and academic anarchy is primarily found on our nation's campuses, but their tribalism has already begun to move out into the whole society. It is clear that the long-term secular attack on the legitimacy of everything from common values to even the legitimacy of scientific knowledge has created an enormous cultural impasse. At present there is certainly no answer to this social incoherence, and it looks like we are headed into a period of disintegration and increasing domestic conflict.

THE EMERGING OPPORTUNITY

In short, recent major social changes appear to restrict our choices of allegiance to two. The first is to continue an identification with modern secular values and the institutions that embody them, such as governments, bureaucracies, corporations, and universities. But as we have seen, the secular ideal is one that is systematically hostile to Christianity — and it is also an ideal that, by emphasizing the isolated secular self, creates the moral crisis of our time. Furthermore, the homogenized secular ideal

---

profound American crackup. When pluralism is understood . as ethnic or racial, Schlesinger clearly grasps the issue and argues against it. But he fails to see how the moral relativity and sexual tribalism of the white American governing class very strongly support ethnic and political pluralism. Indeed, moral pluralism is more endemic in academia than any place else, and it has spread from there to political groups outside the university.

is psychologically so boring — even odious — that it is no longer capable of generating much enthusiasm.

The alternative is the tribal ideal. Here the specifics of race or religion or ethnic identity do provide a meaning that is well worth striving for. But the price is high, for tribalism requires separatism, emphasis on what differentiates one group from another, and thinking that is racist, chauvinist, xenophobic. As people get increasingly disgusted with the very idea of the "average American," who every year represents less and less that is specific, it is not hard to understand the appeal of tribalism. But tribalist logic sooner or later ends in bloodshed and serious social conflict.

Christianity has an opportunity to provide an important answer to this dilemma. After all, the gospel heavily emphasizes how all people are part of the same family. We are all children of God. Christians are found in substantial numbers among almost all races and nations. The universal emphasis in Christianity is so strong that many attribute the same emphasis in secular humanism to the Christian culture from which it emerged. Not only are we all members of the same family, but we are all sinners, we are all called to forgive our enemies, and we are all called to the same eternal life.

Nevertheless, in spite of this heavy universal emphasis, Christianity has been adapted with great cultural specificity all around the world. Christianity in Austria, China, Ireland, Korea, Mexico, Nigeria, Russia, Zanzibar, and many other parts of the world is both rich and diverse. When properly understood, Christianity represents both a wonderful universalism and a glorious particularity.

To say that Christianity has an extraordinary opportunity to resolve this emerging problem is not to say that Christians will live up to the challenge; the Protestants and the Catholics in Ireland, the Orthodox Serbs and the Catholic Croats in Yugoslavia are living proof, alas, that Christians can be far more tribal than faithful to their founder. But nevertheless, the faith offers the opportunity; it is up to Christians to work out the answer.

Index

169